MIRACLES *DO* HAPPEN!

Andrée Virot in the early 1940s

Miracles *do* happen!

Andrée Peel

translated from the French by Evelyn Scott Brown

Loebertas

Published in 1999 by
Loebertas
7 Church Lane, Long Ashton, North Somerset, BS41 9LU

Copyright © Andrée Peel 1999

Andrée Peel asserts her right to be identified
as the author of this work

All rights reserved

ISBN 1 874316 37 6

Typeset and printed in Great Britain by
Loebertas

Contents

Part 1 The Fighting

1	An Invading Army	9
2	Family, School and Country	15
3	Resistance	20
4	Betrayal	36

Part 2 The Suffering

5	Capture	41
6	Journey East	50
7	Ravensbruck	59
8	Buchenwald	77
9	Liberation	87

Part 3 After

10	The Return	93
11	Homecoming, Sadness and Pride	99
12	Family Joys	113
13	La Caravelle	118
14	Lourdes	123
15	An Englishman in Paris	129
16	Student Days	139
17	A Wonderful Gift	147
18	'To another the gifts of healing…'	156

Epilogue	175
Honours and Commendations	179

miracle, n. [Fr., from Lat. *Miraculum* =
something wonderful, from *miror* = to
wonder at; *mirus* = wonderful]
A wonder, a wonderful thing; anything
which excites wonder, surprise or
astonishment; a marvel.

The Encyclopaedic Dictionary, published 1889

Part 1

The Fighting

Chapter 1

An Invading Army

It was the last day of the enemy's successful advance on to our beloved French territory. On this June day in 1940 the Germans reached Brest in the far west of Brittany.

They reached the town gates. The inhabitants had fled the streets as, overcome by despair, they shut themselves up in their homes. A death-like silence covered the town.

Just when I was becoming consumed by an unforgettable sadness, I suddenly heard frantic footsteps on the pavement of our street. I rushed to the window and saw half a dozen French soldiers who were fleeing from the enemy. I ran out to them and stopped them.

"You will be taken prisoners. Come inside," I said. "You must act quickly and get out of your uniform, and put on civilian clothes."

They did act quickly. We ran out at great speed and knocked on every door to beg for clothes so as to save these soldiers. People showed an admirable spirit of generosity at this unhappy time. In a short while I was given everything needed—jackets, trousers, pullovers and so on. Dressed in civilian clothes the men remained free, and they were full of gratitude as they continued their journey into the countryside.

This, my first act of defiance against the German regime, made me wonder whether it was my vocation to fight with the full force of my convictions, and with the help of my complete faith in a civilised ideal. Would whatever I could do make me one of the defenders of Christian civilisation?

But it was time for me to go back to the staff in my shop, a beauty salon which was situated in the main street of the town. To leave these people on their own was not to be thought of. I reached the corner of the street and saw people running to shelter in their homes.

Suddenly a vast number of German soldiers appeared, ahead of the mainstream of the invading army, their motorbikes making an infernal noise. It was obvious that they wanted to clear the street so that they would have it to themselves. With the most brutal arrogance they were pushing people against the walls and ordering them not to budge... Vehicles and troops were arriving all the time. Everywhere faces were frozen with distress. We hardly dared look or listen as we braced ourselves to endure the annihilation of our beloved France. At this tragic time we seemed to feel a greater love than ever before for our suffering country.

I was only a few steps away from a Nazi officer who was policing the streets. He turned to me and said, in impeccable French but with a resonant, satanic laugh, "This upsets you, does it not? We are the conquerors!"

He was making fun of our distress, and enjoying it. My sole response was to look at him with an expression of deep contempt. His cruel words are engraved in my memory for ever. They also revealed something truly unbelievable—the fact that all the invading troops had been thoroughly taught the French language, well in advance, and over a long period, from the most high-up persons right down to the ordinary soldiers. Some even spoke the Breton language!

The long street that ran down to the harbour was green with all these soldiers in uniform who were to be our masters, imposing their laws upon us.

In the days that followed, the more we suffered the more we became proud of our nationality, and the prouder we felt to be French citizens. The days seemed unending, with the dreadful presence of the enemy before our eyes all the time. It was impossible to accept it and one's only escape was to shut oneself in a private world that was impenetrable by anyone, so secure were its barriers.

By the very act of losing our freedom we were able to understand its meaning. It was not just a word in the dictionary with a basic definition; it was not just the ability to do what one wanted to do. It appeared, suddenly, to those of us who had been deprived of it, as possessed of a far wider significance, a quite unique radiance, as of a rare jewel.

Freedom meant, first and foremost, having access to the truth. The day was not far off—in fact it had already arrived—when newspapers would be under the control of our enemies and would be subject to the rule of the lie and distortion of the truth, with severe restrictions put upon the amount of printed matter, so that we were sunk in a sickening miasma of mutilated news.

Freedom means the right to publicise one's opinions and to discuss them and defend them, also the obligation to respect the opinions of others. It means the right to move about without restriction, and this right had been taken from us since we were under restraint from our enemies. Freedom also means the right to bring up children in accordance with their parents' personal convictions, and to inculcate the concept of civilisation that serves both others and themselves. These are such precious values, arising out of Christian civilisation. Whether believers or not, we are all the products of this admirable civilisation with its humane ideals, of which freedom, in its noblest sense, is a most significant element.

It was terribly tragic to lose this precious freedom, but at the same time it gave us the measure of its supreme importance. Until you have been deprived of your freedom you cannot fully understand what it is, or how it permeates your whole life, so that you find you are prepared to give your own life in order to recover lost freedom, and in order to give freedom back to others who have lost it.

Chapter 2

Family, School and Country

My years of carefree youth vanished and were followed by an instant transition to maturity which prepared me for the perils that I knew the future held. One had to find something to go on living for, and we turned our thoughts to a future time when France would not have perished for ever.

There is no doubt that, by my very nature, I was destined always to be a fighter. I was like that at a very tender age, and I am still the same. If any difficulty arises, I immediately bring all my faculties to bear on finding a way of solving it. And whenever there is a battle to be fought for an important cause, I react even more energetically than usual.

These aspects of my personality have always made me seem older than my years, and many a time have I heard my parents say that I never seemed like a child to them.

In our family there was a strong feeling of being French, and we took a great interest in events, political and otherwise, that concerned us. We loved to discuss such things.

At that time, the education in our schools was very efficient. The art of teaching was bound up with the art of awakening in the pupils the joy and excitement of learning. Every week there was a lesson, which was warmly appreciated, in how to live morally and ethically. We were taught how to make our lives useful and how to follow ideals. At the same time we were taught how to face up to difficulties and how to select the most successful way of dealing with them. We were often told about family values, which are so important a basis for society. We learned of every aspect of social behaviour.

These lessons made us fully aware of being French, of belonging to a nation that was just, generous and democratic, that we could admire, and we felt honoured and happy to be citizens of such a country which deserved all our affection.

During the hour's lesson devoted to this kind of teaching, questions were put to us such as 'What would you do if this or that situation cropped up in your life?' We delighted to answer these questions from our personal opinion, and there were times when we surprised ourselves with what we replied.

I remember an occasion when this lesson centred on the subject of the rights of the individual and the citizen, and I was so deeply moved that I wept.

We also used to discuss what frontiers represented. We learned that the frontiers of France were purely territorial, but that, because of our love of humanity, the more we loved France the more we loved all our fellow beings. It was for this reason that France had been given the well-deserved title of 'elder daughter of the Church'.

How much we were indebted to our education when the time came to fight for a noble civilisation, and we found courage to face danger. Thinking of this danger even today I can remember clearly how constant it was, and what immense courage was needed to combat it.

An important element in our sense of duty when up against danger was our patriotism, which was so total and so all-embracing that no dictionary definition of the word could possibly express what it meant. It was the product of an ideal born of noble aims, of a feeling of generosity, and of under-standing what constitutes civilisation, and all this was closely associated with our love of France. When patriotism of this sort is made to suffer through the presence of a conquering enemy hostile to all one's ideals and aims, one's suffering is all the more intense.

And the suffering was made even worse when we thought of the unoccupied part of France where there was a government that had accepted Hitler's rule—and when we actually saw Marshall Pétain shaking hands with Hitler!

I remember one day I was walking in the city centre and saw in front of me a French officer in uniform. I could not believe my eyes. What was he doing in the occupied part of France?

I could not suppress my feeling of disapproval, and my voice betrayed what I was feeling when I said to him: "As you are here in uniform, it is obvious that you have some official contact with the Germans. Seeing your uniform in this part of France is offensive to us, because we are suffering from being controlled by a cruel and hated enemy. In this part of France, many are voluntarily risking their lives by fighting clandestinely, for the love of France and French civilisation."

He seemed to be shocked by this outburst, and he hung this head. I hoped that this was through shame on his part.

Chapter 3

Resistance

A miracle occurred that brought hope to our hearts... Certain French people were continuing the fight in England, and a message came from Général de Gaulle appealing to us to resist:

France has lost a battle!
But she has not lost the war!

The message was secretly broadcast. It appealed to us to set up the Resistance, it is true, but it also acted as a balm for our grief. It did much to strengthen our faith in the future, and there is no doubt that our first action against the enemy was linked with these comforting words.

There were only limited possibilities, because of the number of inhabitants in the city. Together with a few friends we decided to do what we could, and using our typewriter we reproduced the message and turned out numerous copies of it.

Every day, with all the extreme caution that the situation demanded, we slipped these copies through letter boxes.

We were full of hope that the people thus contacted would pass on the message to friends who were suffering the same grief as we were. It was fairly certain that a great many people would soon know of it.

And the day came when, time after time, one would shake hands with somebody, known or unknown, and begin a conversation with the magic words, "France has lost a battle but she has not lost the war!"

One of the first tasks organised by the Resistance was that of clandestinely circulating the 'Secret Press' all over occupied France. This paper carried regular items of news about the struggle against the Nazis, and about what was still being done by the 'Free French' who were in England and had joined in the struggle. In fact, the paper contained anything likely to be of interest to those who were thirsting for the truth. Through this paper we were able to read articles that gave us renewed strength and courage and patience, as well as hope for when we could once again feel proud of our French nationality.

I was in touch with one of those responsible for organising distribution of the paper in Brittany and its surrounding areas. Every time this man came to Brest he enjoyed the hospitality and warm welcome of our house. Fortunately our house was ideally situated in a quiet part of the town. In this street, which was so peaceful that it was a perfect shelter for clandestine matters, there lived a doctor and his family who were courageous enough to give shelter to many British and American airmen who had been dropped by parachute during the various battles. Whenever I think of these people it is with deep admiration.

The organiser of the Secret Press was very appreciative of the security and protection that our house could provide. I knew several people, friends of long standing, whom we could trust absolutely, and they were instructed in the art of exercising utmost caution. They were understandably proud of their brave contribution to the work of spreading information.

It also fell to me to offer the security of our house to a certain secret agent who had a direct link with England, and both received and transmitted messages via his radio. This was always at night, when the windows were curtained to ensure total darkness, as had been ordered by the enemy. The agent would be on the first floor, while I remained on the ground floor listening for a car that used to go up and down the street. It was a German car, and its object was to take note of the slightest sound during the night. From time to time I would lift the corner of the curtain, to make certain that all was quiet. Thank God, the 'danger' kept away from where we were.

At Brest was the headquarters of the French Navy, so information from Brest was exceptionally vital for England. The enemy had access to all the harbour installations and in time would use them in the intense battle against the British Navy, particularly the Merchant Navy. All its submarines were equipped with shelters that were unusually tall, and which could withstand bombardment on account of the great thickness of their walls and ceilings.

In the naval dockyard many men who had been forced to work for the enemy observed things that could be very important for those of us who were continuing the fight. One day a workman contacted me quite by chance to pass on some information, and brought me a stolen document by way of proof. I knew how important this was so I showed it to the secret agent, who then asked me to save all such pieces of information, without fail, because they could be of vital importance. I spoke to the organiser of the underground press, and in due course an agent from England contacted me.

I became Head of the Under-Section and was known as Agent X to preserve my anonymity. In many of the activities of this organisation, prudence was essential. In the specially secret sphere where I was to work, I took the name 'Rose'.

In the interests of establishing the all-important security, I limited my associations to just four other people, and of them each one also knew only four, and so on all along the line. This division of responsibility gave maximum access to the source of any news, which would then be passed back to the centre, namely 'Rose'.

The German Navy and its activities in the harbour installations at Brest were not our only source of information. On the Brittany coast the enemy was busy organising both defence and attack, and excavating rock-shelters on the sea-shore. They were forever adding to these, and we had to note where the shelters were situated and how important they were, and how they might be used for either attack or defence.

Also, our Information Bureau gathered details about the movements of troops and sailors, about the transporting of munitions and materials for reparations, about the arrivals and departures of naval personnel, etc. The enemy could not cover all that they did with a cloak of total secrecy.

It was with difficulty that we got to know the movements of the German Navy. We usually only discovered that they had left the day after their departure. Only once or twice did we succeed in finding out in advance that they were leaving and actually see them sail out to sea. When this happened we were lucky enough to be able to report their departure to our intelligence network in England.

Then came the day when the British aerial bombardments began. They were very frequent, and unbelievably fierce. The enemy lost no time in organising defences, and the roofs of certain houses near the harbour were manned by soldiers. The violence of the bombing was so great that these soldiers were chained to their guns, so that they could not escape the death-dealing hell which was all around them. Sirens would give warning of the arrival of the British bombers, but the population could not heed the warning and go to their shelters, as there were none. Our hearts were full, not of fear but of an unbelievable feeling of gratitude and welcome for those who were risking their lives by continuing the fight while the ordinary people calmly walked on the pavements. I remember seeing, on the pavement, some boys of about thirteen or fourteen who were holding hands and singing: "What joy, Tommy, now we are united at last!" to a well-known tune of the time. Meanwhile the bombs kept raining down!

It was obvious to us that the RAF (which was later joined by the American Air Force) had no wish to bomb the town, but, for all that, houses were often destroyed. I have one memory that can never be obliterated, so much did it mean and so deep was the impression it left with me. After a night when the bombardment had caused serious havoc in the town, my father (who, with my mother, was at this troubled time living in a house in the country) had come to spend the day with me and we went together to the city centre. Crossing a charming square of eighteenth-century houses, we found that one of them had been destroyed in the night.

A man was standing beside the ruins, and he suddenly stretched out his arms heavenwards and cried out: "My God, I thank you with all my heart!"

My father went up to the man. "Excuse me," he said to him, "but isn't that your house—what remains of it? Can you tell me why you are thanking God?"

"Yes, it is my house that has been destroyed. But look over there, beneath that little table that is half collapsed. My radio set is intact and I can go on getting the truth from British radio broadcast!"

My father was very touched, and shook the man's hand. "I understand, and I admire you..." he said. For this man, at that moment, access to the truth was more important than the loss of his house.

One day the Allied bombardment had a remarkable outcome when one of the most important units of the German Navy was severely damaged.

There were hundreds killed, almost all the unit. All the corpses were hastily piled up on lorries which then headed for Germany.

We received confirmation of this from a man who used the customary method of transmitting news, so that I was informed. This man lived near the road, some ten kilometres out of the town, and he had seen a procession of heavily laden lorries. The last of these happened to have its rear door still open, so that he saw the vast number of corpses, still in uniform, lying on top of one another and filling the lorry.

Inevitably, during these intense bombardments the enemy defence forces attacked the Allied bombers. Many airmen escaped by parachute, fortunately a long way from where the enemy was, and families in the area were able to help them and hide them. Our first job was to fold up the parachute and bury or burn it, and then to find jackets and trousers for the men to wear instead of their uniforms. After that, we escorted the men to the houses of people whom we could trust, and whom I shall always remember for the way they gave them hospitality at risk of their own lives. The enemy was totally ruthless, and any family found to be harbouring a British airman would be shot. How can anyone think of such extraordinary courage without being profoundly moved?

Food was strictly rationed during the occupation, and at times there was extreme shortage. We had a real problem when we had to find enough food to feed the English and American airmen. It could be obtained only by means of official individual ration cards, which were distributed at the Mairie, and everything was strictly controlled. We had the good fortune, thanks to someone who worked for us, to enter into a contract with an official at the Mairie who very courageously offered to help us by issuing cards under false names. Also we very often received valuable help from the countryside nearby which was covered by our information service. So we were saved.

Once safely hidden the airmen could tell us their names, which we forwarded to England. We then waited for a code phrase that had been agreed in advance by English radio. One such example was 'the acacias are in bloom'. This phrase let us know that on the next night that there was no moon a submarine would come to the coast and fetch all the airmen back. This was a terribly dangerous procedure as the enemy was frighteningly close to us in the shelters all along the coast. The airmen had to be taken to the exact spot where the submarine would surface. There were very few cars available, and often they had to cover the distance on bicycles, following one of us who led the way. Usually a big house would shelter us until nightfall, and then the airmen would make their way cautiously to the coast. Now very close to freedom, they had to get into two or three black boats launched on to the water from the submarine nearby. The pitch darkness of the night, once every month, gave them an uncanny protection. All went well, and success was total every time except on one occasion when the sea was turbulent and one of the boats capsized.

I was walking in the town one day when suddenly I saw in front of me one of the English airmen who should have been repatriated. He recognised me, and he could speak French well enough to tell me how the stormy sea had caused the boat containing him and four companions to capsize. They had been picked up by a fisherman in his boat, and the fisherman's son had driven him by car into the town so as to contact me. It was a miracle that had led him to me as he did not know where I lived.

The presence of an unaccustomed black boat on the beach had attracted the attention of the people living nearby. The fisherman's son told me that people were more and more inclined to imagine things, and this meant very real danger.

I weighed up this danger and what it could mean, and wondered what was to be done about it. Could anyone force people to maintain silence, and absolute silence at that? I had an idea, and decided to contact the only person who might be capable of compelling such a silence, namely the priest at the little village church. I asked him to listen to me for a few moments while I told him why it was imperative to act swiftly.

"I beg of you, before God, in this church, to give me your solemn promise to keep secret what I am about to tell you," I said.

Then I revealed to him how it was that the coast near his village was being used for the repatriation of English airmen who had been shot down during the aerial bombardments. But how was he to make his parishioners observe the same silence?

It was afternoon, he said, and the bad weather meant that the fishermen were prevented from going to sea, so everyone would be at home.

"I'll go and ring the church bells. I'll keep on ringing them, and this will be so unusual that I'm sure people will come out and want to know the reason for the bells ringing in that way."

Sure enough, a few people entered the church, and the priest said to them: "Go to every house and say that something terribly important has happened, and all the villagers must get together inside the church as soon as possible."

As soon as the little church was full, the priest made his announcement.

"Something has happened that is of vital importance," he said. "Several people may well be risking their lives. I ask everyone here to hold out his hand and say 'I swear before God that I will maintain complete silence!'"

For me it was moving to hear all these people collectively take the vow of silence. The priest then explained to them how the oddly shaped black boat had been wrecked on the beach.

I think that our belonging to the Christian Faith undoubtedly gave us strength and a refuge. Far more people than before were attending Church services and ceremonies. Often, if you went into a church, you found a beneficial calm that gave added courage, and the profound peace seemed to offer the recuperation necessary to gather fresh strength. I loved those rewarding times.

But one day I made a sudden and spectacular exit from the village church where I liked to attend Mass on Sundays. On that day the priest was not the one who usually officiated. He began his sermon in a way that was totally unexpected, by reminding us—to give us more courage, he said!—that we in occupied France were very lucky to have a government with Marshall Pétain at its head, and we should obey his orders... Thanks to him, we had to accept what was happening!

I got up abruptly, and my voice showed how revolted I felt as I shouted out: "Accept? Never!" I made my way to the door and noticed many approving faces as I passed by.

All the priests that I knew in Brest were true Frenchmen who suffered through the enemy's presence in their midst, and I frequently got great benefit from their help. That other one must have come from Marshall Pétain's France!

By that time the fisherman who was sheltering the airmen had done as I requested and had hidden the boat away from enemy eyes. Not another word was said.

When the information that we received took on a more general nature, and when the demand for it became increasingly urgent, we could only deduce that the invasion was imminent. In order to remain in contact with the English Services we went to Normandy. A farmer there whose land covered a large area remote from the enemy's whereabouts had agreed to put at our disposal a rectangle of land of vast dimensions which was surrounded by various trees and dense hedges, so that a small aircraft would be able to land there in safety. We would be there, on the darkest night, all four of us, each person hiding in one corner of the piece of land.

When we heard the low sound of the aircraft engines we all switched on our little electric torches to enable the pilot to see the contours of the area where he was going to land. We handed over documents and received others in return.

It was during one of these aircraft landings that a message from Churchill was transmitted, which moved us profoundly and gave us courage. It read:

> This last mission is the equivalent
> of a victory on the battlefield!

To our great regret, we were asked to tear the message up immediately.

I remember that about Christmas time a magnificent cake arrived with our instructions for work. This was a real luxury for us at a time when we were strictly rationed. There was also a small parcel containing a little woollen jacket specially for me, to help me endure the rigours of winter.

Chapter 4

Betrayal

The repatriation of thirty-two airmen was the last important thing that I did. Then I was warned that a certain agent had spoken during Gestapo interrogations. This man had resisted in spite of torture to himself, but when the Gestapo tortured members of his family before his very eyes he felt he could resist no longer, and he revealed several names, including mine. Once liberated, the members of his family ignored Gestapo orders to keep silent and succeeded in warning several people who were under threat of being arrested. This was how I came to be warned.

Faced with this danger I had to escape immediately, with no delay at all as I had only a few hours in which to act. The principal Paris agent, who had himself been warned, instructed me to go to Paris straight away, together with another Resistance supporter whose name had been given to the Gestapo. I asked one of my staff to tell my parents—who knew nothing of my work for the Resistance—simply that I was in extreme danger and urgently needed to leave Brest.

I was wearing an identification disc and was accosted at the Paris station by a man who told me his number, a number that had already been given to me. He took me to the Police Headquarters, a very important location, where the Head of Police received me and told me what my work was to be in Intelligence. To make sure that I was not recognised, he advised me to turn myself into a blonde, which I did.

I went looking for documents in every corner of the town. It was well known by the Police that if the fighting Germans found themselves forced to leave Paris they would see to it that the town was totally destroyed before they left. Hundreds of Resistants were monitoring every action of the enemy so as to find out whether they were setting up apparatus to annihilate our beloved Paris. This task was beset with almost insurmountable difficulties. But if we could only save part of the town... Fortunately the German general in command of the enemy troops in Paris had such a great liking for our capital that he disobeyed Hitler's orders at the time of the Allied victory, and thus saved Paris. Later, France showed her gratitude by granting him French nationality and making him a citizen of Paris.

What amazing news reached the Police Headquarters! I remember this, for instance: if the Germans were victorious they were going to punish their obstinate enemy, England, by sending to Siberia all men aged between twenty and fifty!!

I was working in collaboration with all the Police officers, who showed a great deal of sympathetic respect for me. Later on I was truly touched to learn that during the several days of battle in the streets of Paris, for the liberation of the capital, the members of the Police Headquarters who were working with the Allies distinguished themselves by their courage. They threw themselves into the struggle, calling out: "Let us avenge Rose!" They thought for certain that my contribution to the work of the Resistance had cost me my life.

Part 2

The Suffering

Chapter 5

Capture

The day came when I was arrested by the Gestapo, who broke into the room where I was staying. An agent had been tortured into speaking, and had given my address. It was May 10th 1944.

In the car in which I was taken to the interrogation, I knew that I was going to have to face the worst and reveal nothing.

I was told peremptorily to sit down. The Gestapo officer at the other side of the table gave me a look in which I could discern the deepest contempt and unbounded cruelty, as well as a total lack of patience. Behind him two SS soldiers were waiting for their orders. On the table, within reach of his hand, were some very primitive weapons—a whip and several sticks, some of which had studded strings attached to them.

The questions began. He shot them at me, one after another, in a harsh, guttural voice, with a pencil in his hand to note down my replies. These were: "I don't know", "I know nothing", "I don't know this person", "I have not organised anything", "I can't tell you", etc. etc. Out of patience, he gave a signal to the SS soldiers who then pushed me brutally into an adjoining room.

"Undress!"

They threw me into a huge metal bath-tub, then used their boots to weigh down my body and keep me under the water. When I was about to expire, they seized me by my hair and dragged me out of the water so that I could breathe. As soon as they thought that my life was no longer in danger, they plunged me in again.

I don't know how many times they repeated the performance before the officer said: "Will you speak or not?"

"But I've nothing to say."

His irritation reached crisis point. He gave another signal and one of the SS soldiers took me by my hair and forced me to kneel while he struck my throat over and over again, knocking me most brutally against the iron rim of the bath-tub. My gullet was displaced to the right and my tonsils were crushed and severed. The pain was atrocious. I was unable to swallow my saliva and I found I was swallowing my crushed tonsils. I don't know how my vocal cords were not destroyed. And I went on refusing to speak...

"We'll see what happens in the next interrogation," said the officer, and he sent me away to the prison in Fresnes.

I was exhausted when they took me to the room where I was to await my next interrogation. There were half a dozen women prisoners in this room. They looked at me cautiously and suspiciously, as it was a known fact that people were being put into prisons who were not really prisoners at all, but who had been told to steer the conversation towards any revelations and suchlike that might be of use to the Germans. These people were nicknamed 'sheep', and I might have been one of these 'sheep' sent amongst them to spy on them.

But when they saw my skin all blackened and scarred by the torture, they welcomed me in the most friendly way, which was consoling for me in the state I was in.

Life in our cell in the Fresnes prison was very restricted. We were six or seven in a room of tiny proportions, so we had very little space in which to move. We had one another's company for comfort. We knew that all of us had worked for the Resistance, but by common consent we decided not to talk about it, even in a low voice, for fear of being overheard through hidden microphones. So we talked about our own lives and about things that had happened to us before our arrest.

We slept side by side on the floor, but our sleep was only fleeting and gave us no real rest. The window was hardly ever opened, and never for long enough, and the air was absolutely unbreathable. Our lungs had to struggle to oxygenate our blood, but it was a losing battle, and this was evident from the look of extreme fatigue on all our faces. I remember the prison's wardress coming in to inspect the place, and when she breathed the fetid air she screamed in horror and put her hand over her mouth, rushing to the tiny window to open it wide.

In what followed, this window was to play an important part, with grievous consequences.

When I was called upon to undergo a fresh interrogation I trembled with fear, as I recollected the ghastly methods that they employed. I made myself as calm as I could, and immediately prayed to God to help me to escape, if at all possible, from this anguished situation.

So I was waiting, seated in a room, when the sound of a door being violently opened made me jump with fright. An SS man pushed into the chair beside my own a prisoner with handcuffs on his wrists and with his arms linked together behind his back. I said nothing, thinking that he might be one of the 'sheep', brought before me to obtain some useful information.

"Are you a Resistance prisoner?" he asked me. Without waiting for an answer he said in a low voice: "We must thank God! The English landed in Normandy the day before yesterday. This is the battle to liberate France!"

I saw tears in his eyes. "Now I can die," he added.

How could I thank him for this piece of news? I shall never forget that moment which gave me courage to face the Gestapo.

The interrogation followed. The same officer with the guttural voice asked me direct questions.

"Your name was given by a Resistant who was arrested. What was your work in Paris? And whom did you know?"

Suddenly I remembered what I had done on one occasion only, something that was of unforeseen assistance to me, and was to be my salvation.

"I'm a person of no importance whatever, and that is why you were given my name. Sometimes I was asked to go into a café—never the same one twice—carrying a newspaper that was folded in two. When I arrived someone would come towards me and hand me a letter, giving me an address, different every time, and I had to hand on this letter to someone else unknown to me. But I did not know anybody. The first person who asked me to perform this service was arrested so that from then on the requests were made by telephone." I made my voice rather naive, so that it would arouse no suspicion.

He called to the SS men: "Next, please!"

At least, I thought that he must have said this—in German—because the next prisoner entered just as I reached the door. I was incredibly relieved as I got into the car which was to take me back to Fresnes, where my fellow prisoners were anxiously awaiting my return. They could see at once from the expression on my face that this interrogation had not involved any torture. I gathered them around me and told them the news that the English had landed in Normandy two days previously. It would be impossible to describe the emotion and joy on their faces.

"Thank you, God!" they cried as we laughed and wept at the same time.

I did not think it right to keep this stunning piece of news to ourselves. The prison had an inside courtyard with buildings on all sides. On the opposite side to ours there were prisoners who were kept ignorant of all news, so that they could know nothing of the extraordinary news of the Allied landing. There was a small stool in the room and I climbed onto it. I was then on a level with the window, and I had the idea of tracing by hand some letters which I would write backwards so that they could be read by the people opposite, if they happened to look. I kept on tracing these words throughout the day. They were words of such vital importance, but would they be seen, I wondered? I shall never know whether any of the prisoners noticed these tracings and interpreted them correctly.

But... the Nazi guards had seen and interpreted them...

Shortly afterwards there was the sound of keys—a sound that has remained in my memory—and the door opened as two SS guards entered.

"Who wrote these signs on the window?"

I could not prolong the silence as that would have meant that we should all get punished, so I came forward and said: "It was I."

They seized me brutally by the arms and hustled me down the stairs to the cellars. They then opened a door in the semi-darkness and threw me inside. The door was closed. There was no light other than that which came through the tiny spy-hole above the door. In this almost total darkness I discovered that I had nowhere to sit except on the floor, which was bare earth, and I had to sleep there too.

I remained in this ultra-primitive state for a whole week that seemed never-ending. I was taken out three times a day for essential purposes, and my food, more meagre than ever before, was put through the spy-hole.

Eventually they came to look for me, by which time I was so weak from all my hardships that I could hardly manage to stand on my feet. Every movement was painful. I was taken back to the ordinary prison where I was welcomed with unforgettable emotion by my fellow prisoners, who knew nothing of what had been happening and had feared for my life.

Chapter 6

Journey East

We had only a few days left at Fresnes, then all the women prisoners were taken into a courtyard. I was separated from the rest, and never knew what became of them.

An SS guard made me get into a train where there were already other women prisoners. After just a few minutes' travelling the train stopped at a siding, where there were some cattle trucks. We were made to enter one of these trucks, which was then very forcefully closed. Sixty of us had a little layer of hay for sitting and sleeping on. There was a bucket in the centre for our natural functions that we all had to use alike. What a horrible journey lay ahead of us!

When the train was full it started to move slowly, but very soon worked up an excessive speed. On the sides of the truck were little portholes, criss-crossed with a number of horizontal strips of wood, so the air, fortunately, was replenished. I rose to say, in my mind, a last farewell to the city of Paris, which was becoming ever more distant on the horizon. The last part of the town that I saw, with great emotion, was the Sacré Cœur of Montmartre. I had a few seconds to look at it. "If ever I come back, I promise that my first visit will be to that Basilica, so dear to the hearts of many French people," I thought to myself.

Then I could see no more, and I sank down on the hay in the small space that was allocated to me for the whole long journey. Where were they taking us in this train that was normally used for cattle? What occupied our thoughts was not so much the loss of our dignity but our concern at where we might be going under these conditions. The most likely seemed to be that we were being taken to a forced-labour camp, or, if not that, to our deaths. From the position of the rising sun we calculated that we were travelling east and felt sure that we were on our way to Germany.

The train stopped from time to time, and at one of the somewhat longer stops we heard German being spoken. It was at that moment that we all, throughout the length of the train, began singing the Marseillaise, our national anthem, which has so much patriotic fervour in its words and in its inspired music. When it was chanted suddenly, by hundreds of voices, in enemy territory, it seemed to resound majestically.

"France has lost a battle, but she has not lost the war!" some of us cried out through the tiny windows. The station platforms were crowded with people whose faces expressed extreme surprise and shock.

It was an endless journey with many stops, both short and long. We imagined we must be nearing East Germany. Already, if I remember rightly, we had been travelling five or six days. The hay which was spread on the floor had none of the flexibility of a mattress, and it was hard to sleep or even to try to sleep on anything so thin. The dry hay pricked my face, so that I tried to sleep on my back and got very little rest in consequence. To make bearable all these things, and especially not knowing our destination, we had to dispel our obsessions and make ourselves concentrate on the past. Even the recent past now seemed a long time ago. However had I survived such a long time, surrounded as I was with danger every day? The risky work that we had undertaken had permitted a surprising number of us to survive, and it was an absolute miracle that my contribution had escaped the notice of the enemy for so long. Was I to conclude that I had been given special protection?

After we had travelled some distance beyond the German frontier our train stopped, and with a brutality that we were beginning to know all too well we were dragged out of the trucks and forced to walk towards the camp of Nuengamme. Was this our destination? Had we reached the place where we were to be interned?

Once we had passed through the camp gateway we were made to arrange ourselves in lines, forming a huge semi-circle. Why did we have to be thus lined up and forced to keep silent? It was not long before this question was answered. We were there to learn something that we were never to be allowed to forget.

For hours, prisoners were horribly beaten and subjected to numerous forms of torture in front of our eyes, to the point where they collapsed on the ground covered in blood, either dead or unconscious. If we closed our eyes so as not to see all this vileness, the SS man came before us and reminded us brutally that we had to watch. The next day, we were taken back to the train.

Many memories come crowding into my mind, and many of them are so painful that they never cease to astonish. This one, for example.

When the Germans were short of labour for their factories they would pick out men and condemn them to forced labour. Their method of recruiting was amazingly quick—in fact it took no time at all. A big lorry would block the street, another similar one would block the opposite direction, the distance having been decided beforehand. People who happened to be walking along the street were stopped in their tracks, then all the men excepting the very old were forced into the lorries by soldiers who pushed the prisoners' backs with their guns. They were bound for Germany. Their families were told nothing and could only guess at what was happening. They would not see their menfolk again until the war was over. This happened in several towns, and one wondered why Brest was spared.

I often think about some news which was unexpected and surprising. It reached me from the port of Hamburg in Germany, via the network of four people that I have described earlier. Very probably, one of the Resistants in the chain had been arrested in the street and sent away to forced labour. But how had this person managed to get the news through from Hamburg? Had he run a terrible risk in so doing? He must have been working on the building of submarines, for he was able to inform us that the Germans were producing a submarine of much reduced proportions that held only two men. This two-man submarine could do unbelievable things, such as going exceptionally fast then slowing down suddenly, and diving down to various depths only to re-surface vertically... and all this without being detected by any of the instruments on board the Allied ships. When it came alongside a ship, at a carefully chosen distance, the tiny submarine could send up any number of limpet mines to damage the Allied vessel and cause it to sink.

We were informed of the approximate dimensions of this submarine, and these we transmitted to England, giving all the known facts. More precise details were asked for, but unfortunately there was a limit to the extent of what we could tell the English.

I remember how, long after the war, my husband and I visited Holland where we had been invited by a colleague and friend of his, and we went to see one of the museums that held souvenirs of the war. The museum was in a park right out in the country, and was very well set up. We were going around, very interested, when suddenly I had such a shock that I just stood still, unable to move. I could not believe my eyes. In front of me was one of those amazing submarines. I took a picture of it with my camera.

Throughout that terribly exhausting journey my thoughts were full of anguish and searing apprehension for the future...

I felt total pity for those men who had been taken by force and sent to work for the enemy. I knew how they felt, and empathised with their physical sufferings as well as their moral anguish and their scruples. No doubt they derived some peace of mind and some comfort when they reflected that it was all the responsibility of the enemy, that they could do nothing against this brutal power. Probably they also thought of their responsibility to their own families in the future, if and when they were able to return and go back to their normal life.

I asked myself how I should feel in such circumstances, and decided that I would prefer to die rather than help to produce armaments that could be used to wound and kill the Allied combatants. I could only pray God to let me choose death, but if death were to be denied me then I prayed that I might be stricken with some terrible illness which would prevent me from being sent to work in a munitions factory. The enemy always selected for these ghastly labours prisoners who were fit enough to be beaten and tortured to get the utmost out of them.

The train suddenly stopped and we wondered whether we had arrived at last. We were still in open country.

"Everybody out!" a guttural voice shouted.

The doors of the truck opened slowly, and an SS Nazi and three uniformed women shouted exactly the same words in the same horrible, raucous voice. Our bodies had sadly become very stiff, so that it was with difficulty that we got down on to the track that ran alongside the railway. We were pushed into lines as soon as they had counted us. We remained there frozen with terror as we awaited our orders.

How contemptuous was the expression on the faces of the guards who had control over our lives! As we got down from the trucks we noticed that these brawny women, who had long ago surrendered all their femininity, were each carrying the emblem of their nefarious profession— a horsewhip, which they brandished from time to time as if to remind us that we were their slaves.

When they had us all lined up, the order came to go forwards. We were not encumbered with luggage as we had been told not to bring anything with us, other than a comb, a toothbrush and one handkerchief. On and on we marched. Each step was abominably painful. But where were we going?

Chapter 7

Ravensbruck

Eventually we reached an iron gate, menacingly tall, which opened. It was the concentration camp at Ravensbruck.

We were soon inside the camp, which was surrounded by very high walls topped with electrified barbed wire. Our hearts were constricted with terror and anguish. We were forced to keep absolutely still, with these women looking at us as if we were cattle. They took down our names. The list seemed endless. The sun burned down on us, adding to our unimaginable weariness. This went on for hours. At times we had to support each other so as not to fall over. I felt more than exhausted, I felt ill.

We were directed towards some long wooden huts, one of which was for us. We went in. The single beds were piled on top of one another and were very basic, the palliasses being a far cry from the comfort of a real mattress. You had to be fairly agile to climb up to the topmost bunk. Only one thing gave us the incentive to get to these beds, however uncomfortable they might be: they did seem to offer us what we desperately needed, which was sleep.

There were not enough bunks to go round, but those women had a way of solving the problem. One of them began shouting from the centre of the hut: "Two women in each bunk, side by side. Between them, reaching up to their shoulders, a third woman lying in the other way round."

The solace of sleep seemed a thing of the past.

The next morning, very early, we heard the same woman's voice shouting.

"Get up, everyone! Take all your clothes off!" (Such sleep as we had managed to get had been in our clothes.) "Follow me!"

Like a flock of sheep we went, in our total nudity, to the centre of the camp. In front of a huge building we had to wait stock-still under the sun which was already getting fierce. Then the door opened. We were so distressed at being seen by the guards without our clothes that it was a relief to enter the building.

We looked at this bizarre place with a mixture of horror and amazement. There were no storeys; the building was empty from floor to roof, and was extraordinarily high. It really was a vast place. Everywhere there were inter-communicating pipes ascending to join others of larger bore. In the middle were keys which no doubt were used to open or close the pipes. Uniformed SS men used their habitual weapon, cruelty, to make sure that we were not hiding anything. When they had enquired which country we came from, they suddenly pushed us towards the exit.

Later, when we saw lines of prisoners go into this place and not come out, we realised that we had in fact been inside the gas chamber where so many prisoners were made to die a horrible death. We supposed that the SS had been given to understand that we were not the ones they were expecting. But this was pure guesswork, and we never found out the reason. But we thought that we had escaped the worst.

On this subject, some prisoners from another hut told us something very moving. A convoy destined for the gas chamber had arrived at the camp, and a long, silent column of people was pushed towards the building. They knew where they were going but were absorbed in their thoughts, and possibly their prayers, and simply went along in astonishing silence. Prisoners on their way to work walked alongside them for part of the way. Suddenly a woman who had been condemned, who was living her last moments, began howling uncontrollably.

One of the prisoners who happened to be passing the line of people was a nun with a distinctive sign next to her prison number indicating her religious status. She hurried over to the woman who had lost control of herself, and spoke to her.

"The important thing is to show our executioners that we know how to die with dignity."

Whereupon she pulled the woman out of the queue and took the place herself. One just can't think of words that are adequate to express one's admiration for such an act.

Our hut, or 'block', as it was called, had emptied of many of its occupants, so that we were each allotted a separate bunk. I slept next to a lady doctor who had been a member of the Resistance. But she shut herself away in perpetual silence, communicating nothing of what she was thinking.

In charge of each block there was a woman (one of the prisoners) who had offered her services to the Camp Commandant. As a volunteer for this work she had taken lessons in how to impose silence, how to maintain discipline and give orders, and how to repress any potential rebellions. Her weapon was cruelty, if necessary. She was called the Blockova. It was horrible to think of anyone learning the basic elements of cruelty on all levels, with the object of obtaining predictable reactions from other human beings. Our Blockova was a French-speaking Pole; we noticed how often her behaviour seemed to soften when she was speaking our language.

The day after our arrival we heard the sound of a siren, which seemed strange as we associated this drawn-out sound with air attacks. But the day after that, when we were sunk in the deepest sleep we had enjoyed for many days, this same sound of a siren woke us up abruptly.

"Wake up!" screamed the Blockova. "All of you get on your feet straight away!" It was pitch-dark night. Surely it could not be time to get up?

"Hurry up! All go out!"

"Where are we going?" several voices were asking. We received the usual reply in the usual hectoring voice. We obeyed orders and went towards the door in this night of darkness. We were lined up in groups of ten and made to keep our lines straight. Prisoners from other blocks were also assembled in groups.

Every Blockova was shouting. "Now then, head up! Look straight in front of you! Arms at the side of your bodies! No movement permitted!"

This was our introduction to the morning roll-call. Having to keep still at such an early hour, and for probably four or more hours on end, made us terribly tired.

In due course the word *"Achtung!"* meaning "Pay attention!" was shouted at us by the Blockovas, and meant that the SS officers were coming for the daily inspection of the prisoners. This did not happen till daybreak, around five o'clock. Often during roll-calls the weaker of the women fainted, or simply fell over when they could stand up no longer. Their neighbours would pick them up and keep them on their feet in such a way that they were hidden from sight. Usually the sheer number of prisoners provided a shield that kept them out of sight of the Blockovas. If they happened to be so close that they could be seen, a well-aimed blow with the horsewhip was enough to awaken the unfortunate fainting women.

When the roll-call was over we returned to the block through a small room where everyone received a cup of coffee and a piece of bread.

My health was not of the best. In fact, I was about to get a merciful granting of my prayer that I might suffer a serious illness that would prevent my being recruited for work in a munitions factory. I have called this granting of my prayer 'my first miracle'.

I was beginning to have increasingly violent pains in the cervical vertebrae and at the base of my skull, on the inner side of my ears. These symptoms were accompanied by a very high fever, and I was told that my face was a deep crimson. My ability to think or to remember anything diminished with every moment that elapsed, until I lost those faculties altogether.

The doctor who was my neighbour at night told me that I had a typical meningitis caused by a virus—actually 'foot-and-mouth' disease. This virus is usually carried by cattle and I had probably picked it up on the cattle trucks. I was told afterwards that when the doctor placed a napkin soaked in cold water on my forehead the napkin became quite hot in a few moments.

I was in a semi-comatose state, and suffered enormously from being unable to express myself. My mind was almost totally dead, but I was aware of two things: firstly, the place where I was; and secondly, the great kindness with which I was surrounded. I had to be present at roll-calls and was firmly held up on both sides by helping hands. A prisoner in front of me who was physically stronger than the others managed to hide me when the SS men came to inspect us. And there were in the block some Polish prisoners who were very clever at getting the Blockova to ignore my illness, which they assured her was only something transitory. My life was saved through the kindness of all these women who, thank God, succeeded in shielding me and hiding me and keeping me from the gas chamber. By rights I should have died.

One day, a slight improvement set in and my strength began to come back. Then all that remained was the pain within my ear. This too became less and less, but that part of my recovery was much slower. With the progressive improvement in my health, my memory also returned. Meanwhile my physical strength was slowly but surely returning all the time.

I could not do nothing so I was given the job of fetching buckets of water to wash down the block and the refectory. When I considered what I had escaped, such as being taken to the building where prisoners were forcibly seized to be used for medical experiments of extreme severity and without anaesthetics, I realised that I had been granted a miracle in more than one way.

After the prisoners had been working for some while in the munitions factories the time came when we were to leave. Ravensbruck supplied personnel for other camps which were short of labour for nearby factories.

But we could not stop thinking about all that we had experienced in this Camp of Death. What unforgettable memories we should carry away from this place, where millions of prisoners had been massacred, killed in that gas chamber, or horribly tortured, and where none of us could escape the smell of death. What would our memories be? We should remember the skeleton-like beings who had been imprisoned for years, without doubt; it was almost impossible to distinguish the dead from the emaciated living. Their striped clothes hung upon them and flapped around their thin bodies. Their status was reduced to a number on their sleeve and a letter to indicate their country of origin. If I remember rightly, mine was 32,920F, a sign that thousands had preceded me.

The striped blue and grey dress caused a profound repulsion in me which has never left me in all the subsequent years. I can't bear to see that kind of striped pattern in fabric of any sort, whether clothing, household drapes, or whatever. I can't look at it without feeling a kind of malaise. 'The striped ones' we were called, and by that name we recognised one another.

Moreover, this garment and a pair of knickers were the only clothing we had to protect us from the vagaries of the climate and the hideously low temperatures of the Siberian-like winter that we had to endure. Just imagine whole months elapsing without our being able to see the windows in the block—hidden as they were by at least twenty centimetres of ice, possibly more... Then we had to stay outside, without moving, for the endless roll-calls. To survive all this you needed to have a tough constitution reinforced by an iron will that was determined to go on fighting and not to surrender to death. Many of the older women, sadly, could not stand up to the appalling daily ordeal... Fortunately we did have shoes, rather like sabots with thick wooden soles, which prevented us from stiffening up totally while we stood in snow that often turned into ice. We had to fight this icy cold and get the better of it! The temperature fell to -30°C during that winter at Ravensbruck.

What other memories should we have of our stay at Ravensbruck? The food, if you could call it that. In the mornings, after the roll-call, we had a cup of coffee which was supposed to warm us up, with about twenty grams of bread. At mid-day we had to fetch a kind of round dish, of no great depth, for our soup. This dish had lost all its enamel, and was so repulsive that one would hesitate to feed a dog out of it. Once we had the dish we joined the long queue, hoping that the soup would be thick enough to appease our hunger and hot enough to make us feel warmer. There would be a piece of bread with the soup. In the evenings we were given two small sandwiches containing two slices of uncooked sausage. With every meal we had cups of water or very weak coffee. How was one to survive on such an ill-balanced diet, which did no more than just keep us alive, our bodies getting thinner and thinner?

One day, to our great astonishment, we were each given a raw carrot. This was part of a generous parcel for the prisoners, sent by some Swiss people. We learned afterwards that such parcels had been arriving regularly, with pulses, pasta, rice, etc. for the prisoners, but they had been kept by the Nazis for themselves and their friends and relatives. But for us a humble carrot was a luxury. I wonder whether this is the reason for my particular fondness for this vegetable?

There were many outstanding horrors, but of these there was one that reached an all-time low of disgustingness. It affected some of the prisoners in our block. They were made to stand about thirty yards from a Nazi guard, who then turned his back on them and forced them to kneel with their heads touching the ground. They had to move in closer, and any prisoner who resisted received so many savage blows from a horsewhip that she became totally exhausted and had to obey, after being forced to eat some excrement that a dog had recently left on the ground. The SS guards were so pleased with their victory that they laughed loudly and raucously. It is beyond imagination that anyone could do these things and get such vulgar pleasure from doing them.

Often during roll-call a wagon full of corpses would pass by on its way to the crematorium, whose tall chimney belched out thick smoke and filled the air with a smell of burning flesh that hung about for a long time. We knew that the farmers were buying the ash to spread on their fields. Perhaps this was the reason why the crematorium worked overtime in the spring?

Before we left for the next camp we were subjected to a medical examination. This was a series of tests carried out with the habitual brutality. They were past masters in the art of cruelty when they were dealing with their slaves. I could only think that a nation that had trained these executioners, and that had so much suffering and death on its conscience, a nation that had so diabolically and systematically engineered those monstrous tragedies, had forfeited all respect. One might be able to imagine an occasional German who had attained true moral heights and had led a blameless and praiseworthy life, but however innocent such a man might be his nation had lost our respect. It could only be a source of shame to be born German.

But how can one explain a miracle that occurred in the midst of all these horrors? As long as I live this miracle will remain with me, together with my admiration and gratitude for having my life saved.

For some time we had had to attend the roll-calls in a different part of the camp. It was an area of greater length, which reduced the number of rows of prisoners. This meant that the Nazi official who was carrying out the roll-call could more easily control the rows. He had more room in which to move about.

Certain Polish women in our block had befriended me and helped me. They had not fought as Resistants, but it was obvious that they hated the enemy just the same. They belonged to the aristocracy of their country, which was the reason why they had been arrested and brought to Ravensbruck. They were very friendly and civilised, and they spoke impeccable French. They liked talking to me. When my health had improved somewhat, we used to have some very interesting conversations.

During one of the roll-calls the Nazi official moved along more slowly than usual, and was watching the rows of prisoners very intently. His gaze lighted on me; I was in the third or fourth row. He had obviously detected something that displeased him, for he kept his eyes riveted on my face. I wondered whether he was perhaps one victim short on the file he was compiling of us. A soldier put this file on a little table.

"Take that woman's number!" he shouted, lashing out at me with the end of his horsewhip. "For the gas chamber!"

The soldier stepped across the rows of prisoners and twisted my arm violently so that he could read my number, which he wrote on a sheet of paper in gigantic numerals. Then he placed this on top of the names that were already written down, on the table which stood about half-way along the length of the roll-call area. I was filled with an unforgettable anguish. I was living my last hour; everything was coming to an end. No hope of ever seeing my family again, or seeing my country being liberated... All was to vanish as I died this ghastly death... By now the SS were only thirty yards away from me.

Then suddenly, in the midst of my despair, I was amazed to see one of the Polish women whose friendship I so valued throw herself almost to the ground. She cautiously crossed over the rows of prisoners, slipped along until she reached the table, and quickly snatched up the piece of paper with my number on it. She did all this without being seen by the SS, and returned to her own place undetected. What else could she do to save my life? She ate the sheet of paper so as to leave no trace... My face was streaming with tears. My life had been saved by a miracle of heroism that no words could possibly describe. This supremely brave woman had risked her own life to save mine. Thanks to God, her wonderful stratagem had succeeded... I could not find words to express my admiration and gratitude. This second miracle has always had an important place in my poignant memories, and inspired within me such heartfelt gratitude that I felt an obligation to make my life in the future worthy of having been saved.

Very soon after that the Polish women were sent elsewhere, and I never knew anything of what happened to them after Ravensbruck; I had no idea whether they were alive or dead. But I have always felt that that admirable lady was my Good Angel, a benevolent spirit that has been with me then and now and forever.

When the day came to leave Ravensbruck we were rounded up in our hundreds, all along the hutted camp, facing yet another of those interminable waits in a state of great discomfort. After several hours we finally set out to walk several kilometres to a train that was waiting for us. This time it was a goods train that we were to travel in. We were crammed as tightly as possible into each compartment, with two Nazis armed with automatic rifles keeping a watch on us. The doors of the compartment were left open as the train travelled along.

The Nazis pointed their weapons outside the compartments. At first we did not know why, but when the train began making frequent stops, of greater or lesser duration, we began to understand the reason. Prisoners could escape by slipping out of the compartments and running off, especially at dusk or after nightfall, and the Nazis had torches with which to light up the darkness. It was their responsibility to see that the right number of prisoners was kept on the train.

When we were passing through Berlin the doors of the compartment were abruptly closed. Anyone who could get near the tiny windows with horizontal bars was able to see that the city was a heap of ruins. The Allied bombings had achieved their aim.

Finally we reached Leipzig. We were made to get out of the train beneath a rain of blows from horsewhips, while howling dogs kept us in serried ranks. We were in the suburbs of the town. There were factories everywhere, in amazing numbers, and hutted camps to accommodate the prisoners necessary to work in them. One group at a time the prisoners were allocated to a hutted camp, while the rest of us moved on. I was in the last group.

Chapter 8

Buchenwald

The long rows of hutted buildings constituted the Buchenwald Concentration Camp. Here we were given a new number, which was fixed on to our clothes. My number was 4217.

The next day we were sent to the factories. I was last in the queue of prisoners. A woman in Nazi uniform came up to me and asked me in a harsh voice but in excellent French: "What were you doing at Ravensbruck?"

"I fetched buckets of water to serve the needs of the block. I was made to clean the block and the toilets."

"You'll do the same here. We need two or three prisoners to clean all the blocks."

The miracle was still manifesting itself! Once again I had escaped from having to make munitions. I felt brave enough to put up with this sort of work, arduous though it was. Although there would be little chance of rest, I considered myself very lucky.

We communicated very little amongst ourselves as we had a constant sense of danger, but somehow word went round that, as far as possible, prisoners were slowing down their work. This was their first attempt at sabotage, and they also used other methods—more and more of them, until these acts of sabotage seemed beyond their control, contributing enormously to raising self-respect as the prisoners succeeded in winning this special battle of wits. The German staff in the factories did not employ brutal methods. Both male and female prisoners (the latter being only a small number, occupying one block) were allowed to work with reduced supervision. These prisoners were too precious an element to be ill-treated.

But the whole framework of the camp itself was Nazi, and everything went on in the same way as before, with the usual cruelty. As an example of something all too well known by the prisoners, one of the Polish women did not on one occasion wake up early enough to be present for the morning roll-call. She arrived running, and the female Nazi officer screamed abuse at her then lunged at the unfortunate woman with repeated blows of her horsewhip. The prisoner's face was so badly injured that it was soon covered in blood so that she was unrecognisable. After the roll-call almost the whole of her face was hidden behind a thick bandage put on by the nurse who was attached to the factory. But the next day, when she again had to present herself to roll-call, this Nazi ogress snatched off the bandage and redoubled her blows to that poor woman's face.

Some of the prisoners could not bear this refinement of cruelty, and began to protest. One of them was taller than the others, and the Nazi monster ran over to her and struck her brutally. Unable to restrain her very understandable anger and feelings of revulsion, the prisoner returned the blow! To protect the ogress, a Nazi commandant ran to the Frenchwoman and threw her to the ground, kicking her in the face and dealing out a frightening number of blows with the horsewhip. It was horrible. Covered in blood and totally inert, she was pushed forcefully down a long flight of stairs where her body bounced on every step. What became of her? We did not see her again. But she showed exceptional courage in striking the torturess, and to the rest of us she had earned our undying gratitude for having thus taken her revenge.

Very often, French soldier prisoners who were doing forced labour in the fields would cautiously come up to the electric barbed wire fence that surrounded the camp. Very quickly, in just a few hurried sentences, they would give us news of the advance of the conquering Allies. I was granted a favour. One of my friends among the women prisoners asked whether there were any Bretons amongst them.

"Yes, one from Brest," was the reply.

"Is it possible for you to send the occasional letter to France?"

"Yes, if it is very short and carefully worded."

"Please tell Doctor X that I am happy to say that Rose is well, and ask him to tell his mother."

I heard later that this message had been received, and had relieved the anxiety of my parents and given them hope.

We were able to gauge the Allied advance because of the frequency of the bombardments. For days on end we heard the battle raging in the distance. The noise became louder and more intense with every day that passed, so that we could conclude that the Allies were advancing all the time. Then suddenly we became aware of more powerful bombing than we had ever heard before, and the bombs were directed non-stop to exactly the same place, in exactly the same direction. We learned that the town of Dresden had been completely destroyed. But it was only some time afterwards that we learned that the Allies had destroyed Dresden with the precise object of ending the war.

From our block we could see in the distance, at the top of a steep hill, part of the city of Leipzig. By day and through the night bombardments of the most important areas of the town became ever more frequent. Unfortunately some of the factories and some of the blocks of the camp were also targets. We took shelter in the staircases that led down to the cellars.

One day something extraordinary happened. Little leaflets, thrown out from aeroplanes, began falling in our midst. We rushed to pick them up.

Take courage, we are on our way!

Beside these words were very elementary maps which had been drawn to show us the position of the Allies. I never had one of these leaflets, which would have been a priceless souvenir to possess.

At the height of the bombardments we prayed God to spare us at this time when deliverance was so near. But still some of the prisoners met their death.

Our faces showed an immense joy at the thought that we should soon be liberated. We sang. We did not any longer even resent the fact that we were always hungry, food having by now almost run out. We were so excited by what was happening and what was about to happen that we could not sleep. But the roll-calls went on as usual, and so did the journey to work in the factories for most of us, except when one happened to have been destroyed. We were becoming more and more like skeletons, and some of us became progressively less able to move. Others could still walk, but with difficulty.

The day came, towards the middle or the end of April 1945—I don't remember the exact date—when we suddenly heard the abrupt sound of a roll-call towards the end of the afternoon. The Blockova said that the prisoners were to get ready to line up to go out. What did it mean? Were they going to empty the camp of its prisoners, for extermination? The term 'lined up' seemed to us ominously meaningful. Those that were unable to walk had to stay behind. Were they to have some special form of extermination? I happened to find myself close to them, and they begged me to hide myself. "Please, please, stay with us for our last moments!"

As time had passed we had become more and more of a closely knit group, with mutual responsibility. If we noticed one of our number falling prey to despair and ceasing to be able to maintain the degree of courage that was necessary to go on living, as soon as we saw the tell-tale signs on her face, we would go over to her, one or several of us, and try to impress on her that we were a band of comrades out to succour one another. We tried to give her strength, to pull her out of her despair by finding words to utter that were redolent of all the values that gave us our own strength, and that had impelled us to fight our battle all along. We used to notice the change of expression on the face of the despairing woman, and the smile returning to her lips. This active comradeship of ours was an immense comfort to everyone, finding its expression in our voices and our affectionate mutual friendship.

I had a certain reputation among the prisoners, for it seemed that I had the knack of finding the right words to say to comfort people, and they often sought me out. How I thanked God for enabling me to be of use on such occasions.

Those women almost unable to move now said to me: "Please stay with us. We know that you will find the right words to give us courage at the last moment." I could do no other than grant their request, and I hid when the prisoners were lined up to go outside the camp, to meet a fate that was unknown but undoubtedly horrific.

We were very indignant to notice that all the Nazi officers had removed their distinctive labels and replaced them with an arm-band on which was written 'Red Cross'. This was in order to save their lives when they came face to face with the Allies.

When the camp had emptied I left my hiding place and went to the women to strengthen their resolve.

The following morning, we heard footsteps. We did not have any doubt that they were the footsteps of soldiers, and they were obviously German—we could tell that from the rhythmic way they were marching on the flagstones at the entrance to the camp. I glanced at them quickly. Yes, there were three soldiers and a sergeant, and they carried guns to kill us with, so that they could obliterate all evidence of the brutal internment to which the prisoners had been subjected.

But I must not forget to mention that a male prisoner had joined us. He told us something that was unbelievable and horrible beyond all understanding. He had the marks on his face. He had miraculously managed to escape, but could not say how. The Nazis, in these final moments, had had only one idea, which was to destroy the block and its occupants. There was no time to make use of ordinary methods of destruction. What were they to do in the little time at their disposal? The prisoners were assembled in front of the block when the Nazis made their choice: they used flame-throwers which they aimed at the prisoners and the block behind them. At this close range the prisoners died uttering dreadful cries of pain, and soon the block was in flames. The prisoner who had, by a miracle, survived to relate this unthinkable horror thought that he must have fainted on seeing the flame-throwers being aimed at them, because he fell to the ground. He happened to be at the end of a row, and his face was turned to the ground, but even so he had received terrible injuries.

But back to our own predicament. Just as the firing squad was drawing near, the telephone rang in the nearby Commandant's office, now ostensibly occupied by the 'Red Cross'.

What we did not know was that one of the women prisoners had hidden herself under the telephone table. Fortunately she spoke fluent German and later was able to relate the conversation to us.

A woman was saying to the Commandant of the firing squad: "The Americans are at the gates of the town. We saw you enter the camp to kill the prisoners. If you want to stay alive spare the lives of these prisoners."

And the soldiers fled!

At the very minute when we were about to lose our lives the third miracle happened. Our lives were saved.

Chapter 9

Liberation

Our escape was like a very emotional rebirth, life having conquered death and annihilation. We were silent as we felt these powerful emotions, and realised the great importance and value of the life that we had been allowed to keep. How can one possibly express all this? One needs to have lived through these moments to be aware of how impossible it is to convey them in words.

The deserted camp was a little world of its own, silent and absolutely calm. We left the block on the first day and went to look at the rooms where the camp commandants had lived. These places were geared to the high ranking of their occupants. They contained comfortable chairs, which were a godsend to those unfortunates who had been condemned to almost total immobility. We visited the kitchens, where we found some food which was much appreciated in our famished state. But no! After a few mouthfuls we could eat no more. Our systems had become accustomed to near-starvation, and to our great amazement we were unable to eat normal quantities of food. How long would this last, we wondered?

I well remember how one day I decided to go out of the camp to enjoy life in freedom, without those guttural voices shouting orders and without the threat of blows cruelly delivered for cruel ends. So I walked slowly on a path that ran alongside a field. The sun was shining. Farther away, on a hill, I saw lilac in flower. It was a strange feeling to be walking along like this, as if the very path existed to give you back your liberty to go anywhere you chose. This is something very difficult to explain.

I noticed some primroses in the hedges round the field, telling me that spring had come. I picked one or two to smell their faint, delicate perfume. It was indeed faint, this scent, but I felt it so intensely and was so amazed by it that I had to hold on to the wall. It became more and more obvious that we had to spend these days re-adapting to life, from the tiniest details right up to much more important matters.

In the course of this first afternoon we were surprised to see three prisoners who had managed to hide away. They made use of very plain gestures to indicate to us that they were Russian and had been arrested in the field where they were working, two or three weeks previously. They were in a remarkably good state physically, by reason of the type of work they had been doing. They demonstrated their pleasure at seeing us by taking each of us in turn in their arms. They hugged me so tightly that I thought my ribs would crack.

On the third day we heard footsteps. I hurried to the door and saw some American soldiers. What joy for us! They came in, and were very polite but also strangely cold.

"Is there anyone here who speaks English?"

"I understand it although I can't speak it very well..."

"Why are you here?"

"We are prisoners."

Their faces hardened. No doubt they thought that we were common-law prisoners who deserved to be in prison because of criminal behaviour.

"We are prisoners because we were arrested by the Nazis on account of our work for the Resistance."

"The Resistance?"

"Yes, we fought voluntarily against the Germans at the risk of our own lives. We were arrested by the Gestapo. It's a miracle that we're still alive."

And I explained, as best as I could, how two or three days earlier the Death Squad had come for us to kill us, and how they had departed before they could do anything.

The American officer who was talking to us now spoke in a voice that quivered with emotion. "Do please forgive us. We did not know."

The next day an American soldier brought us the biggest bouquet of flowers that I have ever seen in my whole life!

The Americans acted with generosity. They did not want to leave us in the camp, and booked rooms for us in a little hotel in the country, where we could await the day of our repatriation. It was a quiet hotel that gave us the chance to rest, which we much appreciated. We thought we should be there only a few days. However, day followed day with no sign of our departure. We tried to cultivate the art of patience, but each hour seemed an eternity.

Part 3

After

Chapter 10

The Return

Eventually we were told that many little bridges on the railway line to France had to be repaired or re-built before traffic could be resumed. Three weeks passed—very slowly, it seemed. But the end was in sight, and in time we were told the date of our departure. A journey on a train full of passengers marked the end of our painful nightmare. We travelled in comfort back to happiness, to be reunited with our beloved country, and our families and friends.

Throughout the journey the train kept stopping to pick up men and women who had survived their stay in the death camps. But there were hundreds, in fact thousands who had tragically disappeared...

At last we crossed the frontier. We stopped at a station in a small village, and on the roof of that station an enormous tricolour flag was flying. Seeing this flag denoting that we were on French territory—reminding us of all that is represented by France with her ideals of *Liberté, Egalité, Fraternité*—and hearing the voices of the local population who had come to welcome the train and were singing the Marseillaise... all this aroused powerful emotion that was so sweet that we could not stop weeping. Our country was greeting us on our return in an unforgettable manner. I was also deeply moved when I saw once again the Sacré Cœur of Montmartre, that holy place which I had promised myself to re-visit, and which promise I fulfilled the next day.

We were very warmly welcomed in Paris. After such a long journey we were waiting for a good night of refreshing sleep. Then the next day, clad in my prisoner's dress, I was taken by taxi, free of charge, to the Sacré Cœur. As I entered this sanctuary I thanked Christ for having granted us this amazing reprieve, and also for His example and His divine guidance as our invaluable aid in life. While I was absorbed in my prayer of gratitude a priest came over to me.

"You are one of those women who have survived the terrible sufferings, and my guess is that you have come here to thank God. Am I right?"

"You are absolutely right. I have been under protection, and my gratitude is boundless."

Then he said: "Because of all you have suffered for a noble cause, you have a duty to pray for those who are asking God to forgive them. Your prayers will be answered."

I felt very humbled, and I answered him in a voice heavy with emotion: "Thank you! Only God knows whether I am worthy or not."

My pilgrimage of gratitude to the Sacré Cœur left me with this touching memory which has always remained with me, and I often think about it.

After returning to the hotel we were taken to a shop and invited to choose a dress. I surprised myself by choosing a black dress that I considered elegant, yet I swear that all my life blue has been my favourite colour!

The time had come for our little group to go our different ways. We made promises to meet again and to keep up the friendship that had united us all in those painful days. We were given a little money—how strange it felt to be dependent on a hand-out! The taxi took me to the station, where a train was ready to depart for Brest. The doors were already closed, but then a window opened in one of the compartments.

"Give me your bag! Lift your arms up!"

Two pairs of masculine hands caught hold of my own, and I was hoisted up the side of the compartment until I reached the window, where someone helped me to climb through. A moment later, the train left for its destination. It was probably thanks to my prisoner's garb that those kind people saw that I was not left behind on the platform.

The train was full. In the compartment people squeezed together so that I could sit down. All faces turned towards me as they plied me non-stop with questions and eagerly awaited my replies. I told them all about what had been happening to me in the so recent past and my travelling companions all reacted with hatred and contempt for that barbarous race.

Eventually they asked me: "Where do you live in Brittany?"

"In Brest."

I saw a sad expression on all their faces as somebody said: "Brest no longer exists. The town is completely destroyed, after a violent battle that went on for forty days."

"But surely the landing took place in Normandy?"

"In Brittany, Brest and Lorient remained occupied by powerful German forces, thousands of men—thirty thousand, in fact."

"But weren't the Allies advancing towards the German border?"

"There were always at Brest great numbers of submarines which were a serious threat to the American Allied forces. The submarines and all the Germans were so active that the Americans decided to attack not just the harbour but the whole town, so as to make life impossible for the German troops. Soon the town was attacked with such force and violence that it became a heap of ruins."

"But what about the inhabitants?"

"The people were warned, by leaflets dropped from the air, that they had just that afternoon in which to leave the town."

"Did the Germans surrender?"

"Yes, in thousands. But there were thousands of dead, on both sides."

So my beloved town of Brest was totally destroyed. What shocking news! What about our house? Had that disappeared? It was fortunate that my parents had their house in the country. That was where I had better go, and I would get off the train at Landerneau, about four kilometres from the house.

Chapter 11

Homecoming, Sadness and Pride

When we reached the town, which was not far from Brest, the station was amazingly full of people standing on the platform. I was puzzled and could not imagine why there were so many people waiting for a train.

A lady hurried towards me. "We are here to welcome you," she said, "to greet you on your return, and to tell you how happy we are to see you alive; also to tell you how we honour you."

"I can't tell you how touched I am by your welcome. Where is my mother?"

"She is waiting for you at your home at La Roche."

"But my father will have come here, for certain. Daddy, where are you?"

All the faces turned towards me, and I saw how troubled and deeply distressed everyone looked.

"We must ask you to be brave, but your father was killed... We have seen your mother this

99

morning, and she wants you to honour his memory by being brave."

I cried out in despair. "How horrible! I can't believe it! I so loved my father!"

The crowds of people fell completely silent in their sympathy and deep emotion.

"And where are my three brothers? Do you know?"

"The oldest is working. Maurice has written to say that he will very soon be back from the prison camp."

Then they were silent again. Why this silence?

"And Fernand?"

"You must feel proud of him. He met his death—a heroic death—in a violent battle on the Rhine."

I could not bear these dreadful blows, for I loved these two persons so deeply. All together we had been a happy, united family, whose behaviour had always been exemplary.

All these people showed me enormous friendship as they tried to help me to bear up through these blows. I felt dizzy and unwell, as if I was falling ill again. I was taken into a house to rest. But I thought of my mother, and how terribly alone she must be feeling, and I prayed God to give me the strength to bring some consolation into her life.

They took me to her. She was waiting for me at the door, with tears streaming down her face.

"Having you with me will give me courage... It's wonderful to have you here..." she kept saying. I found that she had aged greatly through all that she had suffered, and I felt I had to give her all the more love.

I could never have guessed how my father had died. He was fond of walking, my mother told me, and his favourite walk was along the river bank. On the little incline where he happened to be, there was a German soldier trying to catch a fish with a hand-grenade. He threw this, and it exploded right over the river. My father was hit and died immediately.

"I could not have got over this appalling grief," my mother went on, "if I had not been surrounded by so many kind neighbours who rallied to help me and made me go and stay with them for a while."

The next day my one thought was to go to the cemetery which was next to the village church. My father had loved the architecture of this very

101

ancient church. I found his grave with his name and his little *Chevalier de la Légion d'Honneur*. Each year the President of the Republic of France dispensed five such honours across the nation. He had come to inaugurate one of my father's last creations, the Bridge at Plougastel, which was constructed of concrete arches and was of a design that was ahead of its time in its audacity. My father's work was so excellent that the President awarded him one of the five *Légion d'Honneur* certificates.

But on that particular day I found on his grave something that seemed to have been put there specially for me: beside his name there was a superb red rosebud. No doubt the wind had blown this lovely flower over from a nearby rose-bed, but in the memorably emotional state I was in at the time I felt the presence of my father. I felt that I was in his thoughts and that his immortal spirit was all round me at that moment.

Just when one least expects it, past memories come crowding in and we re-live precious moments of our life, which become very real. It is like a sudden apparition from the past, surely proving that the past is really an eternal present. Recently,

I was thinking of my father and all the qualities in him that I admired. He certainly lived for his work, and never ceased to look for perfection in it. When he was superintending the building of the bridge with its three enormous arches—the first of its kind to be constructed in concrete—over an arm of the sea in Brittany, many countries showed a great interest in the new and very daring type of technical skill involved. Some of these countries had requested permission to send their own specialists to observe the techniques. They all came together, including one Russian.

At the end of their short stay they returned to their own countries, but the Russian, before he left, asked to speak to my father. He spoke impeccable French.

"What do you want?" asked my father.

"It's like this: through observing you I have come to regard you very highly, and I want to request your discretion, so as to feel sure that all this will remain a secret. Let me tell you that I was sent by the Russian KGB to steal your plans for this construction, the plans that you were keeping strictly to yourself. If I go back empty-handed I shall immediately be severely punished, with at the very least three months in a prison camp in Siberia where the work will be worse than painful, and I shall be far from my family who mean everything to me in my life. When you go to inspect the work-force I could force this door, or just go in as it is not locked. I could steal all your work plans which are on the shelves inside, and I could disappear with them. But, as I have said, I think highly of you and I cannot bring myself to commit this theft. I do sincerely respect you. Would you please be kind enough to give me two or three out-of-date plans that you no longer need, that would still be of interest? In that way I should avoid the worst happening, and you would not mind parting with plans which are no longer relevant or very confidential."

"I appreciate our conversation," said my father, "and I appreciate your candour and honesty, and the risks that you are running in asking this of me. I never hide anything from my family, so I must tell them about this, but they will be discreet. So here are two or three plans which are not of vital importance any longer and do not apply to the present time."

How had my brother died?

"He died as he had lived," my mother said, "helping others, hurrying to the assistance of anyone in danger. I am so proud of him that I have told myself I must not cry. I will tell you all that I know. The priest sent me all the family photographs that he carried with him, and a little Book of Common Prayer that was found in his pocket."

Dear Fernand. I recalled an unforgettable dream that I had had when I reached Ravensbruck. I was in front of a very steep hill, and I had to get to the top where a wooden barrier separated two meadows. It was a difficult climb but I finally reached the barrier, and I saw on the left slope a silhouetted figure, some distance away. Then I heard a voice, very distinctly, and I knew beyond all doubt that it was the voice of my brother Fernand.

"Andrée," the voice said, "be brave; be very brave. You will have to suffer a great deal, but remember that I will help you and I will carry your heavy burden for you."

Then the silhouette vanished.

Having passed his final exams at the lycée at Brest, Fernand had decided to prepare himself for the Military Academy at Saint Cyr. This was a laborious preparation that could only be undertaken at a Jesuit college near Paris, where the discipline was very strict and the educational standard very high. He came home for the long vacation, but by then the enemy was getting nearer and nearer.

"There's no doubt I shall be taken prisoner as soon as they are in complete control," he said to me one day. "But I shall try to escape them. Perhaps there are still a few boats ready to sail, and perhaps one of them would take me on. What do you think?"

"I agree with you totally. We have no time to lose. Let us go tomorrow morning; we will leave quietly so as not to wake up our parents."

There were only three ships left in the Brest harbour, one belonging to the British Navy and two big ships of the French Merchant Navy. On the quay there were several young men who were trying to escape. One of the ships accepted them, Fernand among them. Soon I saw him on the deck. He shouted loudly so that I could hear him: "I have nothing from my family, nothing to remind me of my life past and present... I beg of you, please get me a few souvenirs. It is not far to our house."

The ship was due to sail at any moment. I have never run so fast! At last I was in the house, wondering what to take, and decided upon some photographs that bore witness to our happy life together in our united family. Then I got my prayer-book, and that I put into a box that I fastened securely with an elastic band. These things were little enough, but time was passing and every second was precious. Even as I ran to the ship the noise of its engines told me that departure was imminent. Fernand was at the same place on the deck, so far above me that I wondered however I could throw the box high enough for him to be able to reach it. But luck favoured us, and he managed to catch it. He pressed it to his heart, as if he were trying to send his thanks to me.

I watched the ship as it moved slowly out and then picked up speed, till finally it disappeared from view. With it went my dear brother who was hoping that fate would take him far away from the enemy. Like me, he thought he was going to England to carry on the fight there. But he was taken to Morocco. We received only one of the letters he sent us, and that was the one he wrote immediately on arrival there. He was at Meknes, a town in central Morocco where he had been offered work in a lycée, teaching physical training. My parents were quite happy at the way things had turned out for him. We learned, long afterwards, that he had been to university, and after three years of study there he had obtained a degree in English.

There had been a landing of American troops in Morocco, before D-day in Normandy. The French army was formed. Anyone with a university degree was made a top-ranking officer, so that Fernand found himself immediately up-graded to 'Aspirant Virot'.

The troops landed at Marseille, where major battles were being fought, and Fernand distinguished himself by his courage in action. He was awarded the *Croix de Guerre*. The troops then began to travel northwards along the Rhône and Saône. This whole journey was beset by murderous battles. When they were about two hundred kilometres from the German border, Fernand had an idea. He mentioned it to the soldiers whom he was commanding. The risks entailed would be tremendous, but all said they would be willing to die or be taken prisoner.

Fernand had their full support so he went to submit the idea to the Colonel of the Regiment, who was absolutely astonished and exclaimed: "You will be heading for death. Nothing like this has ever been contemplated before. I repeat, you will be going to your deaths, all of you!"

"But my men have agreed to attempt this action, with no hesitation; they are prepared to risk their lives."

"If they have really agreed to it, then there is nothing I can do to stop you. May God protect you all."

The audacious plan was to set off at an agreed time, to cross the forest and to march for hours to reach, around midnight, the town where the Headquarters of the German Army was situated. If any place was supremely well guarded, that was it. The Army High Command was protected and safeguarded all round. Whoever would dare attack that? Fernand had planned everything and had thought out carefully how to deploy his troops, and, partly because of the surprise factor, his audacity was rewarded. The senior officers of the German Army were taken prisoners.

The inevitable consequence was that as soon as they were no longer under orders the German troops went over to the French side and were made prisoners. All together they travelled towards the German border, a journey of about two hundred kilometres, with no fighting and no loss of men.

On the Rhine, however, the fighting resumed with terrible violence. The Germans had to defend their country, with all the strength that their despair gave them and with all the military weapons still at their disposal. During this battle a young officer received serious injuries and collapsed next to my brother. Fernand hoisted him on to his shoulders to carry him to the ambulance. Then he was hit by a bullet full on the chest, and it was his turn to collapse. He was beyond recovery, and died a few hours later. Dear Fernand: you have never died in our thoughts and our feelings of pride in you.

The success of this heroic action brought Fernand the posthumous award of a military medal. This is the highest honour, reserved for exceptional merit only, and is very rarely given.

But this award was not the end. There was a sequel that was very moving.

In 1985 my brother Maurice (General Virot) telephoned us.

"Hurry! Hurry! Pack your suitcases! Our brother Fernand is to bestow a great honour on our family, and we have to go to Saumur to be present at a ceremony."

He then told us quickly why our presence was needed in that town. At Saumur there is a famous Military Academy where reserve officers are trained. Each important group of these officers, in possession of acquired information, is called a 'promotion', and each 'promotion' is known by the name of an individual selected from either past or present history. This year the 'promotion' had selected the name of... 'Aspirant Virot'.

In the courtyard of the Military Academy all the officers were standing to attention for the ceremony. There was a general from each one of the Allied countries, and a superb military band. We had privileged seats. In the centre of the courtyard stood the General in Command of the Military Academy, who recounted the whole life story of our dear Fernand. His story had many emotional aspects as it was told. As we looked around us we could see from the expression on their faces how moved many people were. From that time on, throughout their army careers, those officers would wear on the sleeve of their uniform an elongated triangle depicting the emblem of the Military Academy of Saumur, and the name 'Aspirant Virot'. This ceremony proved a lifelong memory for us, of great beauty.

Chapter 12

Family Joys

My mother, with me beside her, was beginning to savour life a little once more. Those days of rest were salutary for me too, for my re-adaptation was very slow. Thinking, and recalling what had happened, often made me extremely tired. I was well aware that I should need a long period of time before I could re-discover every aspect of my personality. However, slow though it was, my progress continued all the time.

At last a message reached us telling us that the return of my dear brother Maurice was imminent. He had been a pupil of the Military Academy at St. Cyr, then a young officer, and in the first battles at the French border he had been taken prisoner. He was to spend nearly five years in Germany in a camp for imprisoned officers. Five years! Fancy having to endure the slow passing of time, the innumerable days upon days... It is hard to imagine the strength of character needed for such an ordeal.

But now, at last, he was there before our eyes. Our joy at being re-united was mutual. What memorable moments those were.

He had come to know a girl, and a tender feeling had grown between them. She had waited faithfully for him, and some time after his return we had the pleasure of attending their wedding. It was a real delight to see how happy they were. They were to raise a large family. They had eight children—five boys and three girls. Four of the boys followed their father's example, and at the present time are commandants in the French army. Jacques (military aviation), nice wife, three sons; Yves, commandant; Francis, happily married, two daughters. Pierre, also happily married and with a little girl, commanded the Foreign Legion in the Gulf War. The fifth is a pharmacist, married with two children.

One of Maurice's three daughters married a commandant, a high-ranking officer who went on to be the youngest general in the army, thanks to his exceptional qualities in carrying out his duties.

Sadly, he was killed not long ago by a speed maniac behind the wheel of a car. We loved and admired this man enormously, and were inconsolable over his death.

The second daughter married a pharmacist and lives in a handsome town in central France. They are a happy couple with their four children. The third daughter is a teacher in a lycée near Paris. She is unmarried.

My brother Robert met a very charming, pretty girl, very feminine, and he married her. They have two daughters. He worked hard, just as my father had done, and, like him, has left memorials of himself in France in the shape of remarkably well-constructed bridges. He too was awarded a prestigious medal for his work. I have every reason to feel proud of my dear family.

Returning again to the time of my homecoming, our financial resources were rapidly dwindling. At the time of my arrest the Germans had emptied my bank account and closed my business. It now became more and more evident that I had to get some work.

Quite unexpectedly I was contacted by one of the most important political parties in Parliament.

Before long there was to be a General Election, and they were asking me to put myself forward as a candidate. They said that I was held in such high esteem that I could be almost sure of being elected.

But I felt strongly that I wanted to be independent. My father, who knew me so well, used to say: "You are not the sort of person who can work under anybody else's orders. Whatever work you do, you must be independent." If I consented to support any political party I should have to follow a line of conduct imposed from above, and so should have no independence left in what I might do or say. I was very honoured to have been asked, however, and so as not to offend anyone I refused on grounds of health, saying that I had still not fully recovered, and did not feel strong enough.

Our good friends showed us great kindness. They often came to visit us and often invited us to visit them. I must have spoken to them about the fact that before long I should have to look for work. Brest was destroyed, and I should doubtless have to go to Paris. I thought, why not have a restaurant somewhere, not too big but well situated and of pleasing aspect? With the help of a good chef, and that of my mother who was an extraordinary cook, I could work up a good clientele.

My friends knew the direction my thoughts were taking and asked me to go to see them, as between them they had decided something which they wanted to discuss with me.

I learned that they had indeed come to a decision. They wanted to club together to provide the money with which to buy a restaurant. And I need not pay them any interest when the time came to reimburse them. All that was needed was for me to go to Paris and look for a restaurant.

I could not contain my emotion. This unexpected, unbelievable help that was being offered to me was so extremely generous, and it had come to me without my having sought it or asked for it... There was no way of expressing my overwhelming gratitude to these kind people who had offered me so much.

Chapter 13

La Caravelle

I had always had a great liking for the *quartier latin,* that part of Paris which has so much beauty and is so attractive because it is embedded in past history. It seems as if the centuries have preserved it specially for later generations to love and admire it and find interest in it. One thinks of Notre Dame on the Ile de la Cité, of that unique treasure, the Sainte Chapelle, the Palais de Justice, the Sorbonne, the Seine embankments, etc. etc.

When the time came to look for a restaurant, I thought it would be asking too much of fate to expect to find one in this favourite area. But luck and fate combined to grant my wish. In a very wide, pleasant street leading to the beautiful Luxembourg Gardens, which were only two hundred metres distant, was a restaurant that corresponded exactly with my dreams. It was called 'La Caravelle', and the inside walls were decorated with pictures of ships—the caravels of the time of Christopher Columbus—very artistically done, with their sails swelling in the sea-breeze.

One of the most unusual features of the restaurant was a huge fireplace, and that also was ornamented with caravels. It was part of the original building, and I could easily imagine how attractive it would be when it contained a log fire with flames going right up the chimney. Some of the walls were hung with beautiful red tapestries. There was a nice bar, a piano, and room to seat forty people. The kitchen was spacious, and beyond that was a small private flat consisting of two pretty rooms.

My mother was given permanent possession of a comfortable room in a nearby hotel, and the owners showed her great kindness.

I had to find a competent chef to enable me to please my clientele. A former Resistance worker who had survived Dachau agreed to look after the bar. A very nice lady helped me to wait at table, and my excellent cook produced special dishes of a very high standard. We had many patrons from among the people who lived in the street, and they soon came to value our meals.

I tried to ensure that the restaurant offered not only a first-class cuisine at acceptable prices, but also a very special kind of welcome. I always dressed elegantly, as if for some ceremony, and I treated all my customers like private guests. If they wanted to chat for a few minutes, I was always there to engage in friendly conversation with them, and they obviously appreciated this.

The news soon spread that I was a former Resistance worker who had been deported to Germany, and as this district had been a centre for the Resistance this had the effect of attracting a great many to the restaurant. Among others, the Head of the Seine District Police honoured me with his custom. Also the Senate, or second political chamber, not far from the Luxembourg Gardens, sent me more and more customers. But the highest honour for the Caravelle was the custom of the Prime Minister himself.

I also had many professors from the Sorbonne, as well as students, foreign and otherwise. Talking of the Sorbonne, I remember a certain doctor who came from Iran (this was a time when the country was trying to modernise itself and to assimilate, as best it could, certain aspects of western civilisation). He had come to Paris for a conference at the Sorbonne, at which he was going to show his audience a certain treasure of inestimable value. Its existence was known, but it was kept well away from prying eyes as it was so very precious and fragile. I was keenly interested in a long conversation that we had after the restaurant had closed for the day. He told me that this treasure was the oldest medical book in the world. He placed it some three thousand years before Christ.

The following morning I saw him come and knock on the door of the restaurant, which was not yet open. He was carrying a large case. I opened the door.

"Remembering our conversation," he said to me, "I thought you might be interested to see this unique treasure."

He opened the case, and I saw a most unusual-looking casket, something truly antique in appearance, with cushions placed all around it. It looked as if it was made of centuries-old leather.

He asked me to sit down, then he swathed me in several layers of very clean cloth and wrapped my hands in two napkins. When he had done all this to his satisfaction, he opened the casket with extreme care. Wearing special gloves he removed from the casket an extraordinary book, consisting of very thick pages of papyrus that were yellowed with age. You could see traces of Arab writing, and on the cover there were a number of letters, some half obscured and others still visible. It was a kind of book of which we have no conception at all, and was nothing like any modern volume that comes to mind. And he put this treasure into my hands for a few moments, before replacing it with the same care in its casket. How honoured I felt to have been privileged to hold in my hands, even for so brief a time, the world's first medical book belonging to so distant a past.

The Caravelle was so successful that I felt rewarded for all the effort I had put into it. One day I received a copy of an article in the American *New York Tribune*, describing the Caravelle as a restaurant where the food was exceptional and the welcome friendly, and so on... It was not long before this resulted in my having a great many American patrons, many of whom kept the address of the Caravelle.

Chapter 14

Lourdes

Among all the memorable events from my time at the Caravelle there is one that is a hallowed memory. I had, some time previously, agreed to act as secretary of the Association of those who had been fortunate enough to return from the death camps. We used to meet from time to time, and these meetings always seemed to strengthen our feeling of comradeship, and made us very happy.

One day, by common consent, we decided to go to Lourdes to bear witness to our gratitude, and to pray for those who had not returned. So I wrote to the Bishop to ask him to reserve a place for us as soon as possible in the never-ending succession of pilgrimages to that place. Our request was granted, and we were given a date. We had time to notify everyone, and nearly all agreed to come, many from the provinces. We had to organise transport and reserve rooms in a hotel. There were about two hundred and fifty of us.

We had the idea of obtaining a large portable lamp similar to those used by coal miners when they are working underground. The purpose was to light it from the flame that burns, day and night, on the Tomb of the Unknown Soldier beneath the Arc de Triomphe in Paris. We had obtained permission to do this, and when the day came we set off for Lourdes, keeping vigil with this lamp so that its precious light should evoke the nation's respect and gratitude.

As soon as we arrived we went to see the Bishop to notify him of our presence.

"How many are there of you?" he asked.

"Two hundred and fifty."

"What do you mean, two hundred and fifty?" he replied with exasperation. "Don't you know that in order to receive a full ceremony a pilgrimage has to be more than a thousand—preferably two thousand?"

"We knew nothing of this!"

"Two hundred and fifty!! It's ridiculous! I can't find words for my anger with you! Two hundred and fifty? No, it's not acceptable. But now you are here your little procession had better leave the town centre at nine o'clock to walk to the Basilica, where the first ceremony will take place. Go to the office for receiving visitors; anyone will tell you where it is."

This harsh, irascible welcome was totally unexpected. That cold voice had given us a shock, and had saddened us. We now had to tell our friends about it.

The next morning our little group of two hundred and fifty went to the departure point in the centre of the town, with our lamp alight to play its own part in the forward march. We looked around us, and were astonished to see a vast crowd of people. All the nearby streets were black with figures.

A gentleman came over to speak to us. "We have heard of your arrival," he said. "The news has spread from door to door. We know that you are survivors from the atrocities inflicted by the Nazis. You have escaped death, and you represent all those who died a horrible death because of their efforts in the Resistance. It is for this reason that the whole town of Lourdes feels duty bound to march behind you. Even the Scouts' Band will be there with you all."

We had been just two hundred and fifty, a small number of people, but suddenly a miracle had occurred. In this town of unforgettable miracles performed by Our Lady of Lourdes, there were ten thousand or more following us and demonstrating their deep feelings and respect as we marched to the Basilica. The rhythm of the marching was punctuated by the music of the Scouts' Band. The Basilica was only just big enough to contain this crowd. How surprised the Bishop must have been!

The local paper got hold of the news, which quickly spread to the areas surrounding the town and throughout the province.

There were two or three of us in our office and people came from all over, even from a long distance away, to see us and talk to us. In their eyes we had been miraculously healed after our appalling sufferings. We answered all their questions, some of which kept recurring.

"How were you able to endure? Where did your courage come from?"

"We were greatly helped by our faith in God. All those who had fought to save Christian civilisation were sustained by their consciences and by the example of Christ, God's messenger, who was willing to suffer so as to give more substance and more importance to his teaching, and to give our lives the great distinction of belonging to a civilisation that was divinely inspired."

Faith not only gives us directives but also sustains and comforts us in times of suffering, and many people who had up until then lived in ignorance of its importance, and had been indifferent to it, suddenly felt a compelling need to embrace this Faith which makes life significant and gives it a profound purpose. These people sought conversion; the priests and the Bishop had to minister to vast numbers of them waiting to be converted.

We went to pray at the Grotto where the Holy Virgin had appeared in a vision, and where miracles often happened in answer to prayer, often clearly seen by everyone present. We had with us a priest, a survivor from Ravensbruck, who was permanently immobile except for his arms and hands. He was a victim of torture, and he was in a wheel-chair. He took Mass on a little table that had been specially adapted for use from his wheel-chair.

A miracle took place in the course of our unforgettable pilgrimage. We saw him get up and walk. We were speechless with emotion, as he was himself. We could only shout, "Thank you! Thank you, Our Lady of Lourdes!"

When we were about to leave we were all gathered together in front of the Basilica, deep in our prayers, when the Bishop appeared at the top of the steps.

"I beg of you to grant me forgiveness," he said. "God was with you. We have never had such a vast number of people converting to the Faith of Christ."

So that was the loveliest of my memories connected with the Caravelle.

Chapter 15

An Englishman in Paris

But fate had something further in store for me, something of very special importance that was to bring about a complete change in my life and a future that may well have been pre-destined...

It was my free day at the Caravelle, but I had left the door half open. At lunch-time two young men entered and took the liberty of asking me whether they could have a meal. By their appearance I judged them to be foreigners, probably English. I could have said to them: "I can't give you a meal today, as it is my closing day. Could you come back tomorrow?" But I surprised myself by saying instead: "Sit down, and I will prepare a meal for you."

"Do you speak English?" one of them asked me, during the course of the meal.

"Not very well, but I can understand it. I learned English at college..."

So then I found that one of them, on returning from the war, had decided to go to university. For the entrance examination he had to learn several subjects, including French, and that was his reason for coming to France. He had been studying the language for almost a year and he wanted to find out whether he could make himself understood, and understand others.

"If you would like to talk to me in French, I can help you and correct your pronunciation," I said.

So this is what we did throughout the conversation. It was obvious that he was immensely interested in this unexpected assistance. Studying a foreign language with only books to help is very different from using that language for its intended purpose—namely speaking it. He was anxious to get the maximum benefit from the opportunity that had come his way. I have to say that one of my cherished wishes had been to teach, and especially to teach a language. I was therefore all the more delighted to do all I could to help him.

The two men were staying at a hotel nearby. The friend preferred to go out and see Paris, so the next day he came alone for his meal, and spoke to me in

English so as to put all the necessary refinement and tact into what he wanted to ask of me.

"Please excuse me. I know I am asking a great deal, but could you possibly give me an hour after your day's work is over, to help me make progress with my French? We could go and sit on one of the seats in the Luxembourg gardens. I should benefit so very much from your help."

I thought to myself that one hour away from routine every day would be a rather pleasant diversion, so I agreed to do it.

He undoubtedly had a gift for languages. He became better and better at expressing himself in French. But sometimes his native tongue asserted itself when he wanted to talk of his convictions and ideas about life. It was a real joy for me to find how much I could understand. I had read many English books and repeated many phrases over and over again, often aloud, as an aid to memory. Now all this was helping me to understand what he was saying. I then began to deduce various aspects of his inner personality that I found admirable. His views were the outcome of a logical mind which he utilised to the full, analysing everything until by degrees he reached final conclusions. Once he reached this stage, he adhered to his opinions with much tenacity.

And it was precisely his serious, thoughtful approach to life that made him so estimable and admirable. He was very generous in spirit, but chose his friends carefully, and was selective as to what or whom he admired. He had noble feelings which showed on his face. I was interested to find how he enjoyed talking, and everything went to show that he had the ability to express himself with ease. He had the gift of natural eloquence. He was rising all the time in my esteem, and because of this my efforts to help him were doubly rewarded.

But the day came when it all had to end, as he had to go back to England. We were both sad as we thought of the day that was fast approaching.

"It is not a final parting," he said. "I shall come back for a month, and I will retain my room in the hotel which is so near. Do you agree to this?"

Of course I agreed! He was visibly moved when he said good-bye to me, which touched me very much. He maintained contact by telephone.

Then came the day that marked the beginning of that whole month in which we were to form a deeper relationship which would turn our friendship into the most intense and profound feeling in the world... We both knew that from now on we were united in a deep love which was rooted in shared values of the highest order... The strange thing was that these values were held in common, in spite of our different nationalities. Our fond feelings grew deeper with every passing day. This is the kind of feeling that transcends the passing of time, as is proved by the fact that right up to the present time our love still reigns triumphant. After over forty years it has lost nothing of its strength and quality.

When that month was at an end, he asked me to marry him.

I knew that I should not be prepared to give up my freedom unless I wholeheartedly admired the man I was marrying. And I did admire the man I loved, from the bottom of my heart.

But I needed a little time for something that was going to be painful. I had to tell my mother and my family of my decision, and I was going to be up against much criticism and misunderstanding.

"Whatever are you thinking of?" they would ask me. "Why marry a student without a job? Why marry a foreigner? Why go and live in another country with so many different customs? You will have to sell the Caravelle. You will be imposing loneliness upon your mother..." and so on.

I also had to meet John's family and discover whether they would give me the kind welcome that I would hope to receive.

My own family were really troubled, and found it very difficult to accept my decision. I patiently tried to get them to understand that this decision did not rest on weak foundations at all. Life had taught me to think in depth before coming to a decision, and I was proof against any superficial attraction that was uncontrolled and unlikely to last. John and I knew that our mutual feeling was of such calibre that we could guarantee its permanence. We both looked upon life with the same intense desire to learn, to admire, and to share...

I had a friendly invitation from John's parents in England, and my stay with them was pleasant and welcoming. It was the same with John's friends. All the more reason to confirm our decision, and at the end of my stay John slipped an engagement ring on to my finger. The date of our wedding was fixed for the near future.

John arrived in Paris a few days before the wedding. I remember that when I introduced him to my brother Maurice's wife, she said to me: "He is very good looking"—*beau garçon* as we say in French. This was extraordinary, for I had never really noticed that he was handsome. But it was true. What was even more true was that my love for him was not based on his external appearance but on far more important values—in fact essential ones—and that was a good omen for its having enduring qualities.

My mother was not surprised to learn of my engagement and approaching marriage. She knew me well enough to realise that I had thought deeply before making the decision, and she was generous enough to rejoice for me in my happiness.

But what was she to do? We discussed the options at great length, and by common consent decided on the best solution. My mother had a house near Paris that my father had built for us. My brother Maurice, a young officer, and his wife and their two children had been very grateful when my mother had invited them to occupy this house. This was a great help to them financially. In the garden of the house there was a garage, and

I suggested to my mother that she should have this garage replaced by a small private house for her own use. If she did this she would have her own home and still be close to her son and his family. My sister-in-law had a great fondness for my mother, so everything would work out for the best.

We had the civil ceremony on one day and the religious ceremony on the next. The civil marriage, in front of the mayor of the Fifth Arrondissement, was fraught with difficulties. The number of documents required was unbelievable, and it had been quite a task to get them all together. They asked for ten different papers, one of which was missing. This could mean that our civil marriage could not go ahead. What a disaster! We did not know what to do.

I determined to think of some way out. I refused to accept that we could be beaten in this way, that there was no solution to the problem. The papers that they insisted on having were connected with the administration.

"Can I telephone? Can you give me the telephone number of the Préfet of Paris?"

The Préfet controls all the Arrondissements of Paris. And by an amazing stroke of good luck,

I happened to know him. I telephoned him and told him of the obstacle to our marriage.

"Don't worry. I'm on my way," he said.

We began to feel hopeful.

"One paper may be missing," he said when he had assessed the situation, "but I know Mademoiselle Virot, and she has my full respect. Nine papers will be quite sufficient to guarantee the identity of both her and her husband-to-be. I ask you to proceed with the marriage."

The next day the religious ceremony took place in a church that had been famous for centuries past. It was here, in the Middle Ages, that pilgrims used to gather for their pilgrimages on foot to Santiago de Compostela, in Spain.

We had planned to have a short honeymoon on the Côte d'Azur, at Nice, and we enjoyed choosing our route by coach so that we could cross almost the whole of France in the course of the journey.

We were full of admiration for the Alps, so beautiful with their snow-topped mountains and wonderful scenery. Then suddenly, it seemed, the landscape changed and before long we were in the sun, surrounded by mimosas with their lovely golden flowers, and palm trees, and there was the sea, so blue... The Côte d'Azur was showing us all its charms.

The sale of the Caravelle had not yet taken place. The restaurant had to be kept going during our absence and one of my customers, who had become a dear friend, stepped in to help us. She had enough money not to need to work, but one of her pleasures was to come and help me occasionally, especially when I had a great number of customers to serve. She was the daughter of a general, and was very elegant and distinguished. She served meals just as I did myself and just as I liked to have them served. She had agreed to be there from morning to night during our honeymoon, so I was able to enjoy all the sweet moments of the holiday with no qualms whatever.

Chapter 16

Student Days

John, who had passed his entrance examination for university, had to go back to England alone and was on his own until the Caravelle found a buyer. That was a wait of about three months. At last, the day came... My mother stayed at the hotel while work was going on at her little house, and the Caravelle was sold.

We wondered what our financial position would be. Before deciding to go to university John had worked in the office of a big pharmaceutical factory. He did not want to be a burden on his parents, and he had had the providential good luck to win a significant sum of money in a competition, which was enough to allow him to study without being dependent on others. And there was enough left over to help us considerably with our daily needs as a married couple. Together with the money from the sale of the Caravelle, this made us quite comfortable. On top of all this, John's parents insisted on helping us. They were planning to move to the countryside, on the outskirts of the town, and they offered us the house they were leaving. Everything seemed to be conspiring to make our lives as easy and pleasant as possible.

We stayed two years in this house in a suburb of Nottingham, where the University was. John obtained his degree but he wanted to specialise further, and succeeded in getting to Cambridge University. As I wanted to be able to take an intelligent interest in his studies, I read widely on the subject so that I became reasonably well informed myself.

I gave French lessons to add to our income. Having a taste for logic, I devised a method of tuition which produced satisfactory results. My pupils were very interested and made rapid progress, and they recommended me to others.

Everything was going swimmingly, and our happiness was totally marvellous. We liked Cambridge, but we went to France for holidays. We used to stay in a beautiful situation in the

Alpine region, in a small chalet that we rented very cheaply from a neighbouring farmer. John took with him many scientific books so that he could study in this wonderfully peaceful environment, where we were surrounded by scenery that we never tired of admiring. The air was so rich in oxygen; the trees were bent down with fruits, so heavy was the crop. Then there was the welcome from the mountain people whose lives were lived so far from the towns.

There are certain specific memories that are all the more enduring because they bear witness to truths extending far beyond their superficial value. Here is one of them.

One day, we heard the sound of cart wheels and the galloping of a horse on the road beside the chalet. The rider was a friendly farmer from the area who was making for the top of the mountain. He stopped to greet us and exchange a few words.

"Where are you going?" we asked.

"I'm going to the point where the forest ends." This would be about sixteen thousand metres in height. "My cart needs repairing, and I'm going to look for a pine branch up there, so as to be sure of having just the right piece of wood for the job."

"Fancy that! Why do you have to go so high? We are surrounded by forests here, and one would have thought that you could find all the wood you needed."

"That is true, but I have a reason for going so high up. At that height the air is never still, the wind blows continuously, and in winter very ferociously, so that the trees are engaged in a struggle all the time and the result is that the wood is very hard and exceptionally solid."

All these farmers who live so close to Nature acquire knowledge which they turn to their use. But as I reflected on this example I was able to draw a parallel with the things that we acquire in the course of our lives, and their influence on our character. I wondered whether a life without struggle and the necessity to overcome difficulties gives us sufficient determination to behave properly. I reckoned that all the terrible sufferings I had endured had acted as a catalyst for me, helping me to struggle and not to be dismayed by difficulties, and to persist in finding the solution that was imperative if I was to win through. It was true that my sufferings and what they had taught me had made me resilient in fighting my battles, and I took great comfort from this.

Was the tree made all the better for its having to struggle? What an interesting symbol it had become.

Here is another memory of this time when we were the fortunate tenants of the chalet in Savoy.

Water, that essential of all life, came to us from a spring in the courtyard which flowed day and night with never-ceasing limpidity. But one day we had a great surprise which worried us very much. The water from the spring was mixing with earth and was coming out brown. We were dependent on the quality of this water and did not know what to do if it became impure. We went straight to the farm, as the owners of the chalet would have to act immediately to restore our vital water supply.

The farmer's wife quite nonchalantly called her son and said to him: "Get a spade, some nails and some screws, and let's go."

When we reached the chalet she pointed out where the water came from, more than a kilometre away on the mountainside. Turning towards us she said: "Will you come with me?"

"Yes," said John to me. "You go, and I'll do some studying while you are away."

I was mystified and wondered what this woman and her son of fourteen or fifteen were planning to do. She carefully followed a straight course, often stopping to look towards the mountain top. After a while she said to me: "Your hair is long; pull out a dozen strands of it and give them to me."

I became more curious than ever at this request. Whatever was the role of my hair in this process of purifying our water supply? She took off her wedding ring, tied my hairs to it and went on again, holding the ring in her finger tips.

"It is there," she told her son. "Dig up the ground there." He did as told, and after a few minutes the pipe appeared that brought the water down the mountain. Two sections of the pipe had come adrift from one another, and had to be re-joined. Some rusty screws had fallen out. It was a quick job to screw the separate portions of the pipe together again, and an hour later our water was as pure and clear as it had been before. I must go on to say that before the earth was dug out the farmer's wife had put in my hand the means by which she had discovered where the water was. I felt the strong pull of the water from beneath the ground.

I was full of admiration. Dirty water had been purified again through human utilisation of its own power of magnetic attraction. What a profound symbol that was. There was a lesson to be learned here. This event emphasised how indifferent most of us are to Nature and how ignorant of the wonders that are all around us, including these strong powers of attraction that can be felt quite easily. Life presents us with many wonderful and awe-inspiring things of which we are all too often unaware.

I asked myself whether my awful sufferings had made me capable of better appreciating the profound joy of life, better able to notice what went on and to get to know more about it, better able to understand things, to discover the sources of beauty, nobility and indeed everything that has interest and significance. I was sure that my ordeal had indeed had this effect.

Our alpine holidays in which John studied so hard came to an end when he finished his course at Cambridge University and obtained his degree. He had become more and more sure that he had an important part to play in the realm of psychology, especially that part of it which is concerned with the vital importance of the brain in all its aspects, including all mental conditions dealt with by psychiatry. His speciality was neuro-psychology and thanks to the assistance of the Professor at the University a place was offered to him at Barrow Hospital, near Bristol. Contrary to the normal trend he remained at this same hospital for the whole of his career, right up to the top grade.

Chapter 17

A Wonderful Gift

I f I had been given the choice of a subject to study at university I should have chosen anatomy. The human being is so extraordinarily complex that it always seems to me the greatest marvel of creation. The body is a masterpiece of amazing precision, an organism whose powers of adaptation are multiple and complex and incredibly ingenious. It is a never-failing source of wonder, and it is our duty not only to admire it but also to respect it.

And at the topmost point in this marvel is the human brain, dwelling-place of the spirit, the real crowning glory of all life. How could the human being possibly be the result of random chance? One is compelled to postulate the work of a Divine Power of creation far exceeding anything that we are able to imagine.

I remember going to Italy with our parents to visit cathedrals, and when we were in Milan we

147

saw a statue of a man showing the whole of his muscular system; he was wearing his skin like a shawl thrown over one arm. I no longer remember whether this statue formed part of the elaborate ornamentation of the facade of this wonderful cathedral, or whether it was simply in the area nearby. But what stands out indelibly in my memory is the emotion I felt when I saw the hundreds of muscles, of differing shape and weight but all perfectly adapted to work together to achieve a variety of purposes at the command of the brain. I remember how that statue taught me that when I decided to walk, my first step set in motion fifty-two muscles!

Why was I so moved? It was not merely because I had been watching the workings of all those muscles on a lifeless statue. I had been imagining how they would do what was demanded of them as if by magic, thus winning the battle against immobility and fulfilling their purpose in life.

So... I was moved because of my interest in and attraction towards the science of anatomy. I wanted to understand more of the complex beings that we all are.

All this was, I may say, a kind of foretaste, or preview, of something that life had in store for me later on, something that is still a part of my life at the time of writing.

I can think of another happening which had the same element of premonition and gave a glimpse of the vocation that I was to fulfil in my later life. Here it is.

When we were at the Caravelle, my mother was a great admirer of the writings of Père Brothier, founder of the Orphelins d'Auteuil. This institution set out to help orphan children to learn a trade. The children were first of all carefully tested to find out where their individual abilities lay, and then they were encouraged to study in their chosen fields until such time as they were able to begin work. Many of them were exceptionally competent. After the necessary number of years they obtained a diploma. When there was an offer of work, there was no doubt that this diploma was enough to guarantee their success at it. You knew not only that their preparation for the work had been of the highest order, but also that their behaviour was beyond reproach. Each term my mother used to give a sum of money to this wonderful charity that achieved such useful results with these young orphans.

Once a year benefactors were invited to a meal, but when my mother received her invitation she was very tired and asked me to reply and to go in her place, which I duly did.

It was a huge house, with each floor occupied by hundreds of orphans. The ground floor was reserved for the numerous workshops where the orphans learned their trades. I visited some of these workshops, all different but all with their machinery in perfect order and well maintained. Others were reserved for more intellectual subjects.

I felt an immense admiration for this charity which assisted those who had been deprived of the chance of a normal life. I was sitting on a seat in the vast courtyard, gazing at the building as a whole, when a man came out of one of the workshops and approached me.

He introduced himself: "I am a monk, and I teach in this workshop. But why are you not with the other guests?"

"Because I have been contemplating this building and thinking to myself that it is the scene of a remarkable degree of mutual aid. In the Christian religion, loving others means also helping others, and this is something that you do in a way that commands all my respect, and all my appreciation of the results you achieve."

"But, Mademoiselle, you too will help others. You will help those who suffer, and you will go on helping them up to the last day of your life. Because of this God will keep you young and in perfect health."

I was astonished to hear these words, and when I spoke I think my voice must have conveyed how astonished I was.

"But why... why have I said these things to you? I don't know you," he exclaimed. "I've never seen you before; I don't know who you are!" As if to answer his own amazement, he said that he thought without doubt it was an inspiration from above, where the Divine Power guides our destinies.

This explanation was an enormous surprise for me, but seemed to satisfy him. I said I would like to visit his workshop and find out what kind of things he was teaching. I was very impressed by my visit, and by his competence.

When I told my mother about my visit and all that I had observed, and how impressed I had been by all that I had seen, we were both very happy to know about such an outstanding charity. But when I told her what the teacher-priest had said we were at a loss to understand these glimpses of what the future might hold. It was all very strange.

It was years before this revelation came to full fruition. But all the time I was beseeching God to make my life of some use, and in particular of some use to suffering people.

Is it another miracle that God has gone on intervening in my life? Once again my prayers were answered in a positive manner. I was to devote many hours of my life to relieving the sufferings of people with severe pains and afflictions. How?

I had been born with a special gift. Very often I could feel a kind of electric current at my finger-tips, sometimes extremely hot, and this current passed out of my hands into the air. When I wanted to concentrate it and intensify it, my wish was granted. The current sometimes manifested itself very suddenly, and would wake me up from a deep sleep. I was to be given proof of its power when I came to apply it to a specific task.

One day we went to see some neighbours after hearing a cry. We found the lady had stumbled on the stairs and had fallen very heavily. She was in great pain, and was groaning from the pain in her hands and arms and the top of the shoulder. Together with her husband, we helped her to sit up. My instinct made me act promptly. I sat beside her and took her hand, which was beginning to swell, and then I moved my finger-tips very slowly towards her wrist. I could feel the intense living power of my electric current, which seemed to keep a millimetre or two ahead of my hand. Then suddenly the current seemed to move vertically, forcing me to stop for a few seconds. I was tired but I carried on, using just the thumb of my other hand. I followed the same route using this power, and again stopped when the force of it began to penetrate deeply. I discovered that the tendon which should have been attached to the bone was no longer attached properly to it. A tendon exists for the purpose of flexing the muscle and ensuring that it can function properly. If it is not attached the muscle loses its flexibility and becomes useless. So I followed the tendon along until I reached the bone and was able to push the tendon towards the point where it had formerly been attached. I had to do the same with two or three other tendons along the arm, with my current making me aware of any abnormality.

The worst pain was in the elbow. The lady could not move it to assist the forearm to move towards the shoulder. My current began exploring the triceps tendon, with no abnormal response. But when I put my hand to the side, my current picked up something very special. It was at the point where the big tendon joins the neighbouring muscle. My current was very accurate. It is an amazing fact that in our constitution parts that are of a totally opposite nature nevertheless work together as if one was a prolongation of the other, their different nature being of no consequence.

What was I to do? I prayed God to give me an inspiration, for it was obvious that the big triceps tendon and the muscle attached to it were no longer working together. That was the main cause of the extreme pain. My hand moved, seeking to find out what could be done; it moved up and down and from left to right, but the current was negative. I moved my hand diagonally from the base of the muscle to the top of the tendon, but got no positive response. But when I bent the arm vertically in the direction of the shoulder, I had an unforgettable reaction. I had to work in that direction, many times over, until my current resumed its normal rhythm.

Soon I was thanking with all my heart that divine inspiration that had guided me, for the lady felt no more pain and was able to move normally. What a memory! My first healing had succeeded, thanks to this vital magnetic current of mine. My future path had opened in front of me as if I had been guided thereto by some divine order that wanted me to succeed. I was to seek out those needing help, so that my life would be useful, and by this means I would be able to thank God for having saved my life, obviously with this end in view.

Chapter 18

'To another the gifts of healing....'

Once people heard of this first success others soon began asking for my help. As it happened we had just decided to have a room built on to our bungalow, with a huge window overlooking a fine piece of country. This became the room where I received my patients, and I improved my technique for helping them with every day that passed, simply through experience. The essential thing is to find out where the trouble originates, and very often this is a long way away from the area where the pain is felt.

It is uncommon, but not unknown, for doctors to come to me for treatment. They are always astonished to see me locate the seat of the pain simply by feeling with my hand. "You must have a special gift," they say. "There can be no other explanation."

I remember one gentleman who came for treatment and explained to me how his knee came to be in such a bad state. One Sunday morning he was walking in the countryside, enjoying his moments of relaxation after a week's work, when he came to a wall. He jumped over this wall without looking to see where he would land. He landed on a pile of stones which collapsed beneath his weight and his leg was cruelly twisted, with painful consequences for his knee. He was not a child, and deep down inside myself I did not feel my usual compassion. He was perhaps thirty-five—old enough to know better than to jump over a fairly high wall without making sure what lay on the other side of it. Only a child could be forgiven for being so extremely imprudent. This reckless jump showed a want of proper respect for the wonderful muscular construction of the leg above the knee. I explained to him all about this construction, which was a work of genius, and I kept on at him hoping that I might make him see that what had happened was all his own fault. Meanwhile I was working hard to repair his knee, which took me a very long time. He listened to me in silence, but when I looked at him I noticed a smile on his face.

"I suppose you work in an office?" I said to him.

"No," he replied. "I'm a doctor." He was smiling because I had been telling him nothing that he did not already know!

"Then you are all the more at fault. What you did was unforgivable," I said in reply. "I hope that this will be a salutary lesson for you."

He was indeed very well aware of the enormity of what he had done. His colleagues had immediately talked of an operation, but he had come to me after noticing the effect of my treatment on some of his own patients. He had come to the right place when he knocked on my door, you could say, for my treatment had a satisfactory outcome.

I have so many memories of my work over the years. They keep coming back to me: many of them are very moving, and many make me smile.

A girl and her father arrived from Wales one day for a healing. I had not quite finished with the previous patient, so I asked them to sit down in the lounge for a few minutes. When my other patient had gone I went to tell them that it was now their turn. But when I saw that the girl was absorbed in reading a book, I invited her father to follow me on his own.

"What is your problem?"

"Sinusitis. I have suffered from it for a very long time, and none of the remedies that I've tried have done me any good."

Thanks to my electric current I can cure sinusitis, and when I had finished, to his great amazement, he was no longer suffering from it.

But, as they were about to go, this gentleman said to me: "Actually the appointment was not for me, but for my daughter. How surprised I was when you asked me what *my* problem was! But what a marvellous cure—I can't believe it! Could you possibly see my wife, who suffers with her back?"

When that lady paid me a second visit to consolidate what I had achieved with her the first time, she told me how one evening, when all three of them were in the dining-room getting ready for a meal, they had heard strange rhythmic noises coming from the first floor. They were intrigued and rushed up the stairs to find their five-year-old daughter beating her head against a cupboard.

"What are you doing there? Why are you hitting yourself?"

"You are all so happy to have been to see Mrs. Peel. I'm the only one that has not been to her. So I want to hurt myself so that I can go and see her, and she can heal me."

I smiled with emotion. In the mind of a child I was much more remarkable than I really am. I had been put on such a pedestal that I felt very humble as I listened to this touching story.

I am always delighted to be of use to those who come in search of my healing, and I can say that they are of all ages. I treat not only adults and old people but sometimes also young children, and a great many adolescents.

Among the latter I am deeply saddened to notice that they are sometimes drug users, especially cannabis. I recognise the characteristic smell which permeates their clothes, their skin, their hair. I cannot stress enough how sad and horrified I am by this. Hundreds of experiments have been carried out world-wide to study the harmful effects of this drug, particularly on the brain and its functions. My husband being a neuropsychologist, and involved himself in these studies, I have ready access to all this research. I have read and learnt much on the subject, so that I have a certain degree of practical knowledge that enables me to try to fight this evil in the hope of getting people to stop ruining their lives in such a destructive fashion.

When I get one of these 'cases'—I had one only two days ago—I focus my mind upon the subject and ask certain questions.

"Have you tried this drug?" The answer is always affirmative, for it is strange, but universal, that cannabis users do not try to hide the truth. They own up immediately.

"How long have you been taking it....?

"What makes you think that cannabis is not dangerous....?"

"Don't you want to know the facts....?"

And when I begin to enumerate the many ill-effects that follow the absorption of this drug, they have to admit that they have suffered these after-effects. I can give them a list of at least a dozen and a half cases that ended in tragedy. Using a drug like cannabis produces a cumulative deterioration of brain function, slowly and progressively eroding the brain as a whole and at the same time causing irreparable damage to the normal workings of that organ.

Inside the brain is the matrix of our intellect, the 'grey matter' which fashions all our mental activities. Cannabis does not actually attack this 'grey matter', so the mind goes on working normally. But cannabis is a very powerful fat solvent which has a terrible effect on the 'white matter' in the brain, dissolving the special fats of which it is constructed. This 'white matter' then decreases at an alarming rate.

The 'white matter' has many functions; for example:

Judgement, will power, moral stamina;

courage, endurance, moral strength;

adaptability—the ability to react to many different situations, a very complex and many-sided function;

the ability to make decisions at short notice;

the ability to carry through any work undertaken, right up to its completion;

the ability to adhere to upright moral principles and to guide one's actions by them;

and all aspects of the personality.

I show these patients a list of more than eight hundred and fifty studies that have been carried out on the various consequences and different aspects of cannabis. They begin to recognise the progressive weakening of their own personalities, often to a point of no return. What a price to pay for the so-called 'pleasures' obtained from the indulgence in this drug! To induce a slow, steady erosion of health and a loss of mental life in this way is nothing less than a crime.

Often these young people are university students. With great sincerity and determination they say: "I must give up!" "I did not know all this!" "I must stop!" I hope they keep their resolutions. Often after several weeks they telephone or visit to assure me that cannabis is now a thing of the past. I wonder whether they succeed in convincing the 40% of university students who are guilty of this crime not only against themselves but also against their country which has a right to expect better of them.

Whenever I succeed in obtaining the result that I desire, I reflect how fortunate I am to be able to do this work. Many others have the ability and knowledge to be able to exert a good influence over those needing help, but sadly they are often outside the swim of life and lack the necessary contacts. I am grateful for the circumstances which have made it possible for me to try to persuade others to improve themselves; without them I would never have known the joy of getting positive results.

Shortly after I began the work of healing, I decided that I ought to add to my gift by widening my knowledge. I needed to know more about cause and effect, I felt sure of that. So I studied, for example, the importance of food in all its aspects— the role of food of all kinds; the mechanism of digestion; the consequences of food not digested, or not fully digested, passing with its toxins into the blood; the wise balance of food in every meal, and the consequences of dietary errors. I read many books and enjoyed my reading as I became more and more keenly interested in the subject. Far from being a chore, it was for me a real pleasure to discover all I could about our physical and mental well-being, and what was good and what was bad for it.

I noticed that many patients suffering from digestive deficiencies had very pale complexions which did not glow normally. This is difficult to explain... Often, too, I could pick out those who were smokers—not in every case, but usually.

One day, I remember, a gentleman who had heard of me from someone whom I had successfully treated knocked on my door. He taught at one of the colleges in the town. In an unfortunate fall he had knocked his shoulder, and was in such pain that he could not move or sleep. As soon as I saw him come in I decided that he suffered from a disorder caused by the imperfect digestion of dairy products.

"Excuse me," I said to him, "but do you have a peculiar and persistent pain, a kind of burning sensation, in this area of the stomach and bowel?"

"How do you know that? You are absolutely right. I have had this pain day and night with no let-up for three years. I've tried everything: X-rays, remedies galore... Nothing has helped."

"I shall start my treatment of your shoulder by examining your hand, and as I work I will explain what I mean.

"Dairy products are not digested in the stomach but in the bowel, through a special digestive juice secreted in the pancreas—one of five juices that this gland produces. If you don't have this essential juice you cannot digest cheese or milk or anything based on milk. These substances remain undigested, and accumulate in the bowel where they cause inflammation of the lining, which is painful. Also, as it is through this lining that digested food passes into the blood, your blood must contain all the undigested matter with its toxins. This results in great fatigue, and destroys your joy of life, including your mental life."

I reached his shoulder and sized up which parts had been injured in his fall, and I put back what had been displaced. His pain ceased, and he could move his arm and shoulder again. However, I felt that I ought to see him once more to consolidate the repair.

"Can you come back in ten days? And don't eat any cheese during those ten days, or any other dairy food."

"Certainly."

Ten days later he paid me the promised visit.

"How can I thank you? You were right," he exclaimed. "After suffering ceaselessly for three years I have lost the pain. It is marvellous!"

"In everything one must begin by considering the cause or causes. I am so pleased to see that you are free from the pain."

"But I must tell you what I have felt it my duty to do." He went on to explain that he had been to see the Head of his college, where he taught science to fifteen and sixteen-year-olds. He told the Head how his severe pains had disappeared, thanks to my understanding of what was causing them. He now realised that one important thing was missing on his course, and he was going to rectify this. He was going to include 'the mechanism of digestion' as part of natural science. The Head understood perfectly how his conscience had led him to make this decision, and asked how many extra lessons were involved. "Three or four," he had replied, "but I shall devote all my free time to studying the digestion and its mechanism."

The Head sympathised, but said he could not pay him for all the extra hours of work as the budget was already settled for the year. My patient didn't mind not being paid, however, as he was simply obeying his conscience.

After he had spent some time studying the subject, he put the fruits of his labour before his students. It was not difficult to read the less-than-welcoming expressions on their faces. They could see that they were to be given more work to do, and they did not like the prospect. There was a disapproving silence that could be felt.

But he explained to them that he was not getting paid for these extra lessons, and that he was doing them because his conscience made him do so.

So he began his instruction. When he reached the end of his course of four lessons a girl rose to her feet.

"I want to thank you on behalf of all my companions," she said. "We have found the subject very interesting, but we would like more."

To satisfy them he went on to prepare two lessons on the effects of alcohol. The same girl got up again.

"Thank you again," she said, "but still we would like more."

He wondered what to prepare this time that would capture their interest.

"Prepare a lesson on drugs—cannabis, for example," I said to him. "Come and see my husband. He is a brain specialist and knows every detail of the dreadful effects of cannabis on the brain and the personality."

My husband gave him as many guidelines as he could, together with copies of research studies proving the terrible consequences of this criminal habit.

Two lessons served to acquaint his pupils with all the awful dangers of the drug. The girl spoke yet again.

"All our thanks for these lessons and what they have taught us. We wanted to thank you with a present of some sort, an objet d'art, a book, or some such thing. But we could not agree about the present until one of the boys had an idea which we all, with no exception, accepted enthusiastically... " At this moment all the students rose and stretched out their hands towards their science teacher, saying aloud: "We swear before God that we will never take drugs for the whole of our lives."

When this gentleman next came to visit us, he said to us: "When I heard the chorus of voices making this solemn vow I could not hold back my emotion, and I wept in front of them. It was the nicest, most unforgettable gift that I could possibly have had."

We were very moved ourselves to hear about this unusual present.

One could say that we are a vast chemical factory that is constantly at work. The study of the effects of food on our bodies provides us with irrefutable evidence of what gives us good health, what causes disease, and even what creates dangerous arterial hypertension and stress. It is usually possible, without using drugs, to lower the tension of high blood pressure simply by strict control of the diet. But many people, one must say, find it much easier to take medicines...

I remember a lady who came to see me after a painful fall in the Alps, where she had been skiing on a dangerous slope. There was a ring at our doorbell. I went to open the door and found myself confronted by this person.

"I am sorry, your name is not in my appointment book. But do come in."

"I have not come for treatment, but I specially want to ask your opinion. I went to the doctor yesterday, and he took my blood pressure. He told me my blood pressure was very high, in fact dangerously so, and he wanted to give me medicine to bring it down. I tried to explain that I dread taking medicines, as I have a great fear of their side-effects, and would prefer a natural cure. However, he said that my blood pressure was so high that he had to act immediately. There was no time for delay, and he would give me a prescription.

"I told him that I knew he was acting in good conscience, but that I thought a few more days would not matter. I wanted to think about it.

"I cannot explain my total aversion to medicine," she went on, "but I can't bring myself to take any, and that is why I have come to ask your advice."

"But," I replied, "I am not a doctor. I can't take on such responsibility. The decision will have to be yours and yours only."

Then she spoke in a way that I can only describe as inspired. What she said was so simple that I was deeply touched.

"If you were me, what would you decide to do for yourself in similar circumstances? Please tell me."

How could I bring myself to turn a deaf ear to such a request? "I should begin to control my diet, and I should go on controlling it very strictly," I said.

I looked at her. Her face had an expression of desperate longing and expectation, and I prayed God to inspire me to act for the best. I requested a quarter of an hour of my patient, and asked her to sit down while I wrote out for her on four sheets of paper the menu for every day, breakfast, lunch and supper, eliminating all harmful ingredients and carefully balancing the foodstuffs in reduced quantities, with no meat, no fat, and no salt etc. After four days she was to recommence the sequence.

Five or six weeks later, I was again surprised to find her ringing my doorbell. I wondered why she had come back, and I asked her in.

"I have come because I feel I have a duty to tell you this... I decided to visit my doctor, and went to him yesterday. He asked me whether I had been taking the medicine, and he took my blood pressure.

"'Oh, I must sit down!' he said suddenly when I told him that I had not taken the medicine.

"'Doctor, you are not well—are you ill yourself?' I asked him.

"'No, no... but your blood pressure is normal, and I can't believe it! What have you done?'

"'I have simply changed my diet completely.'"

I remember—in fact I could never forget—one patient who had been suffering for years and had given up hope. He had come for treatment without any expectations, but, thank God, he eventually attained complete relief and the treatment was a total success.

The success itself is sufficient reward for me, but I did expect to be warmly thanked by this particular patient. As it was, I could not believe what I heard him say.

"You must not... do you hear me? You must not..."

As he repeated these words his voice became more and more shrill, and he sounded strangely dictatorial. I looked at him in amazement.

"What is the matter? What have I done?"

"You must not ever die!!"

I smiled, feeling much moved. He had expressed his feelings in such an original manner that his gratitude went straight to my heart.

Epilogue

My deep conviction is that I am the beneficiary of a divine inspiration which guides my hands to help to cure those who suffer. It is not my own merit at work. I thank God daily for the gift He has bestowed on me.

Often when I reflect on my life, which was miraculously saved and which has been blessed by true happiness as well as by better health than I could ever have hoped for, I say to myself: "Why me? Why not those whom death claimed, who did not survive to get their just reward later on? Why should I be so privileged?"

On certain occasions when I am asked to represent France I wear the medals that have been awarded to me. I wear them for all those who deserved to win them by their sacrifices and their heroism but did not live to tell the tale.

Andrée Peel
1999

Honours and

Commendations

EXTRAIT

du DÉCRET en date du 25 FEV. 1966

publié au J.O. du 2 MAR 1966

portant nominations dans la LÉGION D'HONNEUR.

ARTICLE 1er sont nommés dans l'Ordre National de la Légion d'Honneur

AU GRADE DE CHEVALIER

DÉPORTÉS - RÉSISTANTS

Armée de Terre

. . . .

VIROT (Andrée, Marthe), épouse PEEL, ex Sous-Lieutenant des Forces
    Françaises Combattantes.

          " Magnifique agent de S.R. agissant en territoire
" occupé par l'ennemi à partir de janvier 1941, a contribué
" à infliger des pertes à l'ennemi par l'excellence et la
" précision des renseignements qu'elle recueillait. A déployé
" une activité débordante outre son action d'agent de S.R.
" dans la diffusion de la presse clandestine et le convoyage
" d'aviateurs alliés.

          " Arrêtée par la Gestapo en janvier 1944, elle
" suscita l'admiration de ses bourreaux par le mutisme absolu
" qu'elle opposa. A été déportée en Allemagne."

          Cette citation annule la citation à l'Ordre du
Corps d'Armée attribuée par Décision n°140 du 20 Avril 1947.

. . . .

          CES NOMINATIONS COMPORTENT L'ATTRIBUTION DE LA
CROIX DE GUERRE 1939-1945 AVEC PALME.

Par le Président de la République   Signé : Charles DE GAULLE
    Le Premier Ministre
Signé : Georges POMPIDOU

    POUR AMPLIATION
L'Administrateur Civil Hors Classe BERT   LE MINISTRE DES ARMEES
    Chef du Bureau des Décorations   Signé : Pierre MESSMER
P.O. Le Chef de la Section "Invalidité"

CITÉ A L'ORDRE de la DIVISION.

VIROT, Andrée - D.G.E.R. F.F.C.

" Agent de renseignements et de liaison d'un S.R. opérant en
territoire occupé. Volontaire pour toutes les missions dange-
reuses, a toujours fait preuve de courage et de sang-froid.
Arrêtée par le Gestapo le 10 Mai 1944, a été déportée en
Allemagne, libérée le 13 Avril 1945."

CETTE CITATION COMPORTE L'ATTRIBUTION DE LA CROIX DE GUERRE 1939 AVEC

ETOILE D'ARGENT.

PARIS, le 12 Novembre 1945.

Le Général DE GAULLE, Président du Gouvernement
Provisoire de la République Française, Chef des Armées.
P.O. Le Général JUIN,
Chef d'Etat-Major Général de la Défense Nationale
signé : JUIN

PRÉSIDENCE	MINISTÈRE DE LA GUERRE
DU GOUVERNEMENT PROVISOIRE	
DE LA RÉPUBLIQUE FRANÇAISE	FRANCE COMBATTANTE

PARIS, le 12 Mars 1946.

Référence à Rappeler:
334.0456 JC-ST

COPIE CERTIFIÉE CONFORME

Le Capitaine LIXER. COULBOIS,
Chef du Bureau Liquidateur des Réseaux
de la France Combattante ;

RÉPUBLIQUE FRANÇAISE

•

Guerre 1939-1945

CITATION

DECISION N° 140
-:-:-:-:-:-:
LE MINISTRE DE LA DEFENSE NATIONALE

CITE : A L'ORDRE DU CORPS D'ARMEE

V I R O T Andrée - (F.F.C.)

" Magnifique agent de S.R., agissant en territoire
occupé par l'ennemi a partir du Ier Janvier 1941, a contribué
a infliger des pertes à l'ennemi par l'exellence et la précision
des renseignements qu'elle receuillait a déployé une activité
débordante autre son action d'agent de S.R. dans la diffusion de
la presse clandestine et le convoyage alliés d'aviateurs.
" Arretée par la Gestapo en Janvier 1944, elle
suscita l'admiration de ses bourreaux par le mutisme absolu qu'elle
opposa. A été déportée en Allemagne.

CETTE CITATION COMPORTE L'ATTRIBUTION DE LA CROIX DE GUERRE AVEC
ETOILE VERMEIL

POUR AMPLIATION   Fait, a Paris le 20 Avril 1947
Paris, le 24 Juin 1948   Pour le Ministre de la Défense National
l'Administrateur de I° UL et par Délégation.
BAULET, Chef de Bureau"   Le Colonel JOSSET
Décorations "   Délégué Général
P.O. Le Capitaine LAMOTTE.des Forces Françaises Combattantes de
                                 l'Intérieur.

RÉPUBLIQUE FRANÇAISE

Modèle 326-2/2

MINISTÈRE DES ARMÉES

DUPLICATA

SOUS-DIRECTION DES BUREAUX
DU CABINET

BUREAU DES DÉCORATIONS

Loi du 4 février 1953 (I. O. du 5 février 1953)

Nº d'inscription

13-29?

CROIX

DU COMBATTANT VOLONTAIRE

1939-1945

Par décision nº ....2956.............. en date du ......4 septembre 1967

le droit au port de la Croix du Combattant Volontaire a été reconnu à

Madame VIROT Andrée épouse PEEL

A Paris, le   4 septembre 1967

Pour copie conforme
~~XXXXXXXXXXXX~~
A PARIS, le 29 décembre 1995
~~XXXXXXXXXXXXXXXXXXXXXXXXX~~
Le Chef du Bureau des Décorations.

Le Ministre des Armées,
Signé : MESSMER

Marie Dominique PERETTI
Attaché principal d'administration centrale

182

LE GOUVERNEMENT PROVISOIRE DE LA REPUBLIQUE FRANÇAISE

Sur la proposition du Ministre de la Guerre,

Vu l'ordonnance No. 42 du 9 Février 1943 instituant une Médaille de la Résistance Française,

Vu l'ordonnance du 7 Janvier 1944 relative à l'attribution de la Médaille de la Résistance Française,

Vu l'avis favorable de la Commission de la Médaille de la Résistance Française du 11 Oct. 19

DÉCRÈTE

ARTICLE 2 — La Médaille de la Résistance Française est décernée à :

Melle Andrée VIROT,

ARTICLE 12 — Le Ministre de la Guerre est chargé de l'exécution du présent décret qui sera publié au Journal Officiel de la République Française.

Par le Gouvernement provisoire
de la République Française
Le Ministre de la Guerre
Signé : DIETHELM

FAIT A PARIS, le 15 Octobre 1945.
Signé : DE GAULLE

BUREAU LIQUIDATEUR DES RÉSEAUX
DE LA FRANCE COMBATTANTE

65, AVENUE GEORGES MANDEL
PARIS (16e)

Référence à Rappeler
334 6814 id/JC-ST

MINISTÈRE DE LA GUERRE

PARIS, le 19 Mars 1946

COPIE CERTIFIÉE CONFORME

Le Capitaine XXXXX COULBOIS,
Chef du Bureau Liquidateur des Réseaux
de la France Combattante

MINISTÈRE DES ARMÉES

FORCES FRANÇAISES COMBATTANTES
DE L'INTÉRIEUR

ÉCHELON LIQUIDATEUR
DU RÉSEAU JADE FITZROY
6, RUE DE NAVARIN, PARIS-9e

No

ATTESTATION

L'échelon liquidateur du Réseau JADE FITZROY, des Forces Françaises Combattantes, atteste que, conformément aux prescriptions des articles 3, 5 et 6 du Décret du 21 Mai 1946 (Journal Officiel du 29 Mai 1946),

Mademoiselle *Andrée Virot*

Agent homologué du Réseau JADE FITZROY, remplit les conditions fixées pour l'attribution et le port de la

MÉDAILLE COMMÉMORATIVE FRANÇAISE DE LA GUERRE 1939-1945 avec barrette LIBÉRATION.

Fait à Paris, le *29 Mai* 1948.

Le Commandant Paul FORTIER,
Chef du Réseau Jade Fitzroy,
p. o. l'Officier liquidateur,

N. B. — La présente attestation donne droit au port de la Médaille Commémorative Française de la Guerre 1939-1945 avec barrette Libération (Décret du 21 Mai 1946).

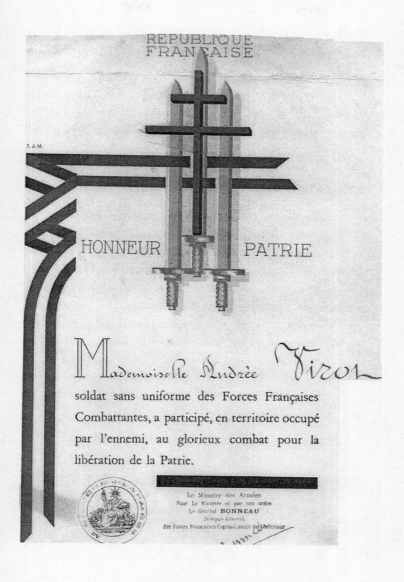

REPUBLIQUE
FRANÇAISE

HONNEUR   PATRIE

Mademoiselle Andrée Vizot

soldat sans uniforme des Forces Françaises
Combattantes, a participé, en territoire occupé
par l'ennemi, au glorieux combat pour la
libération de la Patrie.

Le Ministre des Armées
Pour Le Ministre et par son ordre
Le Général BONNEAU
Délégué Général
des Forces Françaises Combattantes de l'Intérieur

185

CITATION FOR MEDAL OF FREEDOM

Andree Virot, French Civilian,

fought most courageously for the cause of liberty by rendering aid of exceptional importance to members of the American and British armed forces who were evading capture in the enemy-occupied countries of Europe. The courage, bravery, and exceptional devotion to the common cause of freedom displayed by this person in undertaking such hazardous duties, knowing the price to be paid if apprehended, were a definite contributing factor to the termination of hostilities in this theater, meriting the highest degree of praise.

The President
OF THE UNITED STATES OF AMERICA
has directed me to express to

ANDREE VIROT

the gratitude and appreciation of the American people for gallant service in assisting the escape of Allied soldiers from the enemy

Dwight D. Eisenhower

DWIGHT D. EISENHOWER
General of the Army
Commanding General United States Forces European Theater

By the KING'S Order the name of

Mademoiselle Andrée Virot,

was placed on record on

17 April, 1946,

as commended for brave conduct.
I am charged to express His Majesty's
high appreciation of the service rendered.

C. R. Attlee

Prime Minister and First Lord
of the Treasury

By this

Certificate of Service

I record my appreciation of the aid rendered by

Sirot Andrée

as a volunteer in the service of the United Nations
for the great cause of Freedom.

B. L. Montgomery

Field Marshal
Commander-in-Chief, 21st Army Group.

Date 6 Mai 1946
Serial No. 2/144